Praise for *Get Clarity*®

Success in basketball and business constantly challenge the leader or coach to develop a unity and commitment to getting the job done and a strong togetherness to make the team confident and powerful. Guiding talented people to have a strong inner game for themselves and their team is the key to success. Daily situations always challenge our inner game to shift thoughts and negative circumstances into positive energy and motivated possibilities.

The concepts and principles set forth in *Get Clarity* will help you become very clear about what you want—what lights you up. The Clarity tools will keep you vitally present and energetically focused on making it happen. Stay above the line! It works!
—George Karl, NBA Coach

The body of work of Clarity International and the tactics to stay "lights on" in my work and my personal life have created a success habit for me! We "check in" every day, and my husband and I connect on such a deeper and more powerful level with the practices from Powerful Partnering.

—Betsy Wiersma, Author, Speaker
Founder, CampExperience Network

"The Powerful Partnering experience and your coaching has provided us with a playful, useful way of being with each other. This allows us to follow one another's energy and support each of our endeavors while upholding our intention as a couple. We now find ourselves rapidly discovering when we are functioning "under the line" and therefore rapidly recovering to a more effective communication pattern. We consistently remember our visions as partners and individuals and revisit them often – free from fear, arguing or bickering. We more clearly and consciously get and give what we want and need with one another. **Simply put, we feel empowered and have more fun! We get more done with more ease, joy, love and lightheartedness! This is what we knew our marriage could feel like – we only wish we had done it sooner!** We truly feel blessed to know you two. You are a wonderful example that always reminds us to align with one another! Thank you!!!"

—Maggie and Vincent Verderame,
Las Vegas

The fusion of Cathy Hawk's brilliant *Get Clarity* methodology for facilitating personal transformation, with Gary Hawk's remarkable competence in developing the leadership capacity of CEOs and senior leaders, has given rise to this important new book. Don't pick up *Get Clarity* unless you are committed to revealing and connecting with your deepest calling. And if you pick it up, and you treat it seriously, watch out—your life will be SIGNIFICANTLY altered. Leaders steeped in Clarity will ignite extraordinary aliveness and effectiveness in employees in their organizations.

—Barry Heerman, Ph.D., Author
Noble Purpose, and Building Team Spirit

In these times of great challenges and opportunities, the need to lead others and ourselves with wholeheartedness, wisdom, and creativity has never been greater. The guidance system and journey map contained within *Get Clarity* will give you tools and strategies that will have you doing more of what you love and less of what you don't love. Whether you are leading a team of thousands, or a team of one, Cathy and Gary Hawk have laid out a powerful map to light the way. This book will get you there.

—Justine & Michael Toms, Co-founders
New Dimensions Media/Radio, Co-authors
True Work: Doing What You Love and
Loving What You Do

The great knowledge, insight, and inspiration contained in Get *Clarity* are absolute gifts of the highest order.
>—Janet Luhrs, Author
>The Simple Living Guide and Simple Loving

What I learned from the *Get Clarity* process was how to rebuild my life from the inside out. It has changed everything—the way I view people; the way I see and do business; the way I view success and money; the way I view relationships. Every aspect of my life has been improved by Clarity. I originally thought something had to be broken to need this training. What I came to understand was that Clarity's program is especially for businesses and individuals who are performing well, and want to take their business and life to the next level.
>—David Litchfield, CEO & Founder
>Everything Good, Heber City, UT

Thanks to the *Get Clarity* training that we experienced, our entire team has changed the way we work with each other and our clients. The increased focus and energy that our team has gained is priceless.
>—Sue Goodin, Founding Director Progressive
>Health Center, Denver, CO

Most of us may not be able to define good leadership or good partnering. And, we all know it when we see it. In *Get Clarity*, the authors have done an excellent job in defining the role of leadership through partnering. The excellent example stories in this book help show us how we can use the Clarity approach and get better at it; even if we are only leading ourselves.

—Paul A. Riecks, President
Inner Circle Mid-Atlantic

Get Clarity®

The Lights-On Guide to
Powerful Partnering

by
Cathy Hawk and Gary Hawk
with
Theresa Byrne

Books may be purchased by contacting the publisher
and authors at: info@getclarity.com.

Cover Design: Think2a
Interior Design: WESType Publishing Services, Inc.
Publisher: Get Clarity Press
Editors: Theresa Byrne, Joan Duncan Oliver,
Judith Briles and John Maling (EditingbyJohn)

Contents

Gratitude

We are so grateful for all our teachers and guides,
spiritual and human. And we remain grateful
to all the leaders, seekers and lifelong learners who
want to live vibrant, full lives every day.

Foreword

We first encountered Cathy Hawk in December 1998 in Sausalito, California when we personally experienced the Clarity method. Michael recalls being stunned seeing the "before" visuals of his face and then seeing the "after" visuals. The experience was so remarkable that he was catalyzed into a new cycle of his life.

He recalls Cathy asking him the question, *"If you had all your druthers, with no obstacles of any kind, what would you do?"*

Spontaneously he replied, *"I would travel anywhere in the world and talk to anyone I wanted to talk to."*

Cathy then asked, *"Who would be the first one you would go see?"* Michael instantly replied, *"His Holiness the Dalai Lama in Dharamsala, India."*

Within four weeks of meeting Cathy and having this experience Michael received a phone call inviting both of us to attend a special, invitation only, gathering with the Dalai Lama in Dharamsala. This eventually resulted in a private one-on-one interview with His Holiness in his home plus a great deal more. That's what is called intentional synchronicity in the Clarity world!

Justine has had the good fortune of attending the *Get Clarity* retreat training. This intensive retreat downloaded her with the tools necessary to move to the next level of pursuing her work with greater passion and skill. Cathy's river metaphor made a big impression on her.

Justine says: "*When I could see the path mapped out like a river, I truly began to understand the flow of my creative endeavor. I could see the rushing river with the eddies, rapid runs, logjams, and even waterfalls.*"

This helped her to understand that passion and enthusiasm are a large part of the creative process; however, one must be vigilant like a river captain, skillfully rafting down the challenging rapids.

It is our experience that being aligned with one's purpose and direction is the energy that gets you into your river; however getting into the river is only the first part of the journey. Once you are in the flow, you need a clear map with simple and effective steps to assist you in finding answers, create breakthroughs and go into action to stay connected with your passion and vitality.

The guidance system contained within this book will help you answer such questions as: What's next? What can I do to get more vitality in my life? What is my purpose, my calling? When I feel lost, where do I go? As well as finding and following your lights-on flow, it will give you tools and strategies that will have you doing more of what you love and less of what you don't love.

Simply put, you have to continually ask the question, *"What lights me up?"* to get the accurate answers about your passion, and to know the next step on your journey. From our experience it's an exciting and lifelong learning process. This book will help you get there.

—Justine & Michael Toms, Co-founders, New Dimensions World Broadcasting Network, Co-authors, True Work—Doing What You Love and Loving What You Do

Prologue

Pre-Partnership
For Powerful Partnering

True partnership has always sounded amazing and for the right people I believe it can be: in business and in romantic relationships. When I see Cathy and Gary Hawk in action I'm consistently impressed with not only how well they work together but also their great love for each other. They truly appreciate and "get" each other. From where I sit: they are living examples of how true partnership can work in the world.
—Theresa Byrne

It's an honor to help this book get released into the world. It is actually a fine example of another form of partnership: *an alliance of collaboration among the three authors.* What I've learned about partnership through *Get Clarity* training must be shared in the world. It's time we learned a new way of being together and a new way of co-creating. No more compromising as a way to get what we want. We can look to creating a new way of collaborating beyond the old models or paradigms. The world is ready. Are you?

Pre-Partnership Promises

This section covers how to be in the best position to attract and bring in the greatest possible partner for yourself. It is also a great way to attract a fantastic business alliance—the principles for positive partnering are the same.

We are at a time in our historical development/ societal evolution where we no longer have to partner together for survival, as it was just a few generations ago.

We're also at a time in history when two people can both have their dreams come true; we both get to thrive. No one has to sacrifice or compromise so the other person can get what he or she wants. Therfore, it's important for us to get a handle on how to partner powerfully. We learn how to have our two visions merge with this fresh new approach.

Boundaries

What are boundaries?

Boundaries are what you will do and what you won't do; what you want to happen and what you don't want to happen.

The best definition I've come up with after so many years of struggling to explain this esoteric concept while teaching groups is the most simple: *boundaries are the structure we create to hold the things that matter to us the most.*

Things like our energy, time, what we need for self-care, a feeling of safety, our values, wants, needs, desires, efforts, and having healthy, respectful relationships. Boundaries are like the chair you're sitting in right now; holding you up and keeping you stable. The chair is supporting you the way boundaries do once you understand how to utilize them.

Applying boundary practice skills helps you learn to trust yourself, rather than hoping things will just *"work out"*. We aren't typically taught how to develop effective boundary setting skills growing up so we have to learn them along the way; mostly by trial and error. Eventually we learn to honor and provide ourselves what we want and need—after we figure out what matters to us in the first place.

Having good, solid boundary skills also helps you identify the people in your life you can trust, simply by the way they respond to your requests and boundary setting. It seems odd to say boundaries can build trust but they're some of the most telling tools in human interaction you'll ever find.

If you say something like, *"I really don't like violent movies"* and the person you're dating wants to take you to see the newest slasher film, it's something to note. Or if you say, *"I'm gluten free"*, and a new friend suggests a restaurant with fantastic healthy options. It shows a certain amount of caring.

When you meet someone who respects what you want or prefer, or even acknowledges what you've said, it's something to notice about him or her.

Healthy people respect others who respect themselves; and aren't afraid to ask for what they want or need. Let's say you're in a partnership and your partner is upset about something, would you prefer they hold it all in? Or be able to have the ability to share whatever's going on? A boundary is also the ability to have those tough conversations, even when you've got to talk about what's upsetting you. It is typically the place where a boundary was crossed; these are called *courageous conversations* in my work.

Another indicator of healthy boundaries is someone who knows what they need and is capable of asking for it. As if they understand what they need for not just survival, but to thrive, and aren't afraid to ask for it.

Energy Circles

Each of us has our own personal bubble of energy surrounding us. In *Get Clarity* we call it *"our personal field"*. When I teach self-defense classes I call it our *"comfort bubble"* or the *"safety bubble"* around our bodies. And it's important we learn to handle our own fields before we can become great partners.

In a lush sacred garden in Rennes-le-Château, France, I was blessed to be in workshop training with a Templar Knight who described this beautiful way two people can come together.

What he shared was how the energy between two people's distinct fields intersects and creates another energy all together. In the Ichthys symbol (the Christian fish you see on people's cars), it's symbolized by the area where two circles cross, representing the center where the divine masculine and divine feminine intersect.

I call this space between two people the *"Third Energy"* and that energy has characteristics to pay attention to—equally as much attention as how we feel about the other person. In the *Get Clarity* system it's called *"yours, mine and ours"*.

It's important to be aware of the kind of person you choose to be around. You want to be with people who bring out your best, not your worst (or shadow sides). Imagine two people who appear *"on paper"* like they should be amazing together based on how much they have in common, but when they get together it's a train wreck. Their third energy isn't healthy, supportive, or lights-on. It's the opposite and they bring out each other's worst.

As important as it is to be with partners who light you up, it's equally important to pay attention to the third energy.

One + One = 3

There's an old belief/adage that each person puts 50% into a relationship to hold up their end of the relationship bargain. I challenge this. Who wants to be in relationship with someone who only puts in half an effort to something so important? When you're a whole person and you attract another whole person, the two of you together can achieve something greater, something new and unique. The sum total of which wouldn't be created otherwise. That's 3, once again the *third energy* shows up!

It means you're putting in 100% toward your partnership, and you are each accountable for holding your own energy fields.

"You Don't Complete Me." (I'm already complete)

Even though it makes for a great line in a movie, you don't actually need another person to complete you. It's not healthy searching to fill a need inside yourself through someone outside of you. You don't walk around with a *"person-sized"* hole inside of you waiting for the right person to step into it. When you are whole, complete, and healthy you don't require another human being to make you complete.

You are already 100%, even though having an amazing partner adds to your life, it won't make or break your life.

Be as big, bold, and lights on as you can and you'll attract in strength not weakness

How do show you up in the world as you attract in the fabulous partner with whom you can build a future? You show up as the highest possible version of yourself! You live lights-on, vibrating at the highest energetic self you know you can be. When you create out of strength you only get more strength.

Several years ago I fell head-over-heels with an amazing man who happened to be the cinematographer on a television show I was filming. I was living my dream, filming both a documentary and a movie and met a great guy while I wasn't looking or planning! It was my strength and glow, shining brightly attracting in an amazing partner.

Keep in mind, when you attract in weakness or play down your strengths, you might pull in someone who wants a control drama or attempts to fix you. You are not broken; you don't need to be fixed.

Be Your Own Best Self First

We are often shown in movies and fairy tales only after we find our prince or princess we'll live *"happily ever after"*. Who wants to wait to start living until they find a partner? Why put anything on hold until you're partnered? Many people wait to do things they want to do until they find a partner, but it's backwards. Do the things you dream and it could be where you find your partner!

I know people who don't live fully because many of the things they want to do; they want to do them with a partner. Things like buying a house, traveling to Europe, or getting a dog. They want to wait until they find their soul mate to go after their dreams.

What if they started with the living happy part first, added in the *"ever after"* section, and did the work they came to the planet to do? What if they were the best versions of themselves long before they ever attracted in their loving partner? What if they did all the wonderful things they'd like for themselves before they attracted in someone great (and expected that person to take care of them)? What if they instead became two people being their best selves and co-created something amazing together?

You Attract What You Vibrate

How do you know you'll attract the best possible partner? The secret is in living as your highest self and following your own dreams. One of the best pieces of wisdom is to get to know your shadow, or darker side, and accept it (because we all have it).

Make peace with it. Learn to not only live with your shadow side but also learn how to switch your thinking when you find yourself in a lights-off place.

Learning how to live a *"high vibrational life"* takes consciousness and practice but it can be done. It's one of the reasons I love the *Get Clarity* Operating System; which teaches that simple attraction tool can literally transform your relationship with yourself and the rest of the people in your world. You begin to pay attention to your own energy, and you *"own"* your field, knowing it's no one else's job to make you happy. *"Holding your own field is job #1"*, as Cathy Hawk often says. This is extremely powerful! When you can hold your own energy, and you value yourself, you become a very attractive, inviting, interesting person to a great partner.

Attracting (Not Seeking) is Key

Attraction through your own high energy vibration is the single best action to take in seeking a partner, especially when you desire the most compatible partner for yourself. Attraction energy creates a feeling of openness, and an invitation for a person who is also vibrating at the level you are. Using self-awareness and figuring yourself out, you can clear out old patterns or beliefs keeping you stuck. This old energy doesn't fall into the labeling category of good/bad or right/wrong but it's something no longer working for you. (In working with mentoring clients I explain it's energy or a pattern created long ago and it used to work, but it doesn't anymore).

In terms of attracting versus seeking, the more you seek, the more you fall into the energy of *"not having"* or *"looking"* and if you're single this energy can create all kinds of downsides. You can start down the slippery slope of doubt or critical thinking in yourself or in the dating process.

Doubt could sound like:

> *"Am I not good enough?"*
> *"Where's my partner? Why is this taking so
>   long?" "Where are all the great
>   men/women?"*
> *"This dating things SUCKS!"*
> *"I'm not equipped for this!"*
> *"There are no great men/women!"*

And sometimes when you're in *"seeking"* mode what you want stays just out of reach—it stays in the *feeling* of wanting but not having. Seeking can be repelling to others if it's done as a way to search for something outside of yourself to fulfill you. It can feel almost needy, as in: *"I need someone else to complete me/my life."*

Seeking can also take on a task-oriented approach to doing more or doing the *"right"* things more than being grateful for the people who we're meeting, or who show up in our lives. Like a missile seeking it's target. Think of all the dating to-do lists or the "Right Person" lists you can toss out! Look for the right qualities, and how you feel with the other person. That's all you truly need on your "List".

As an example, I once knew a man who called dating a *"numbers game"* and as he was seeking his partner, he was simultaneously dating and having conversations with over 10 different women!

The Danger of "Hunting"

Who likes to be treated like prey? Women used to joke about *"husband hunting"* but it sounds awful. Hunting for a mate makes one of you the predator/hunter and the other the prey. That way of thinking leads to making up rules, playing games, and basically not being honest. It makes a winner/loser and prey. And it's not based on connection, trust, or collaboration but on games, intrigue, manipulation, and control. There's a high level of drama and anxiety when this is happening, and it's a dangerous place to feel safe. Manipulative relationships and unhealthy partnerships would fall into this category. And those are not the kind of powerful partnerships you want to be involved in—the disempowering kind!

Know what you want first

By knowing what matters to you, understanding the power in having loving boundaries, and accessing your ability to ask for what you need in relationships allows you to find a partner who is whole, complete, and respectful. This is different than creating a list of ideal qualities in a mate or partner, it's more like a "Life List". What you need to thrive.

The key is in taking time to pause and truly think,

> *"What's important to me?"*
> *"When I'm at my best, what am I doing"?*
> *"What are the things I must have and what are*
>   *my deal breakers in relationships?"*
> *"What do I need to have in a partnership to feel*
>   *good/safe/peaceful?"*

These questions are about not only supporting yourself by knowing what you want in a relationship, but also what does your body, mind, spirit need to thrive? This is self-care on a whole new level. By knowing it's OK to ask for these things, it creates the container I wrote about earlier. You get to keep yourself sane, safe, and sacred and be in relationships where you are treated with the same amount of dignity as you treat yourself.

PART I

Prepare for Departure

Introduction

*Powerful Partnering is an enlivening dance in which you
co-create together by observing—observing and following
the energy of each other, looking for spirit and light.*
Cathy Hawk

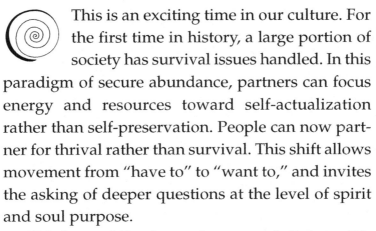 This is an exciting time in our culture. For
the first time in history, a large portion of
society has survival issues handled. In this
paradigm of secure abundance, partners can focus
energy and resources toward self-actualization
rather than self-preservation. People can now partner for thrival rather than survival. This shift allows
movement from "have to" to "want to," and invites
the asking of deeper questions at the level of spirit
and soul purpose.

This huge shift of attention towards living a life
of dreams in partnership with another, presents
many new challenges and opportunities. Although
it's natural in close relationships for energy fields
to become entwined, it is enlivening to learn the

distinction between the energy field of "mine," "yours," and "ours."

To partner powerfully is a call to support and share each other's visions, and to co-create a bigger shared purpose. To answer the call requires the willingness to embrace paradox, reject compromise, and be purposeful. This mindfulness serves the expansion of compassion and peace, health and prosperity that ripples into surrounding fields.

Powerful Partnering is about getting everything you want for yourself while concurrently your partner gets everything they want as well.

It's a dynamic dance requiring the ability to embrace paradox, and reject compromise. You'll learn about energy fields and how they interact. It is natural in close relationships for energy fields to become entwined. You'll soon be very clear about the distinction between the energy fields of "mine," "yours," and "ours."

To be able to support anyone in understanding the distinction of powerful partnering, it's important to understand not only basic relating skills but also the principles of the operating system of *Get Clarity*—as well as what "lights on living" means.

What is "lights-on" living?

Do you have clarity amnesia? Most people do at some point in their life: it seems to be part of the human condition. Sometime during your life you may have lost clear awareness of your purpose and your passions. You lost sight of what gives you joy and energy every day. Forget following your bliss, you weren't even sure what gave you bliss! Things got hazy and foggy. Yet somehow you have never lost a deep, innate knowing it's critically important to wake up and know why you are here.

What is your contribution to the world?
How can you make a difference with your own
unique expression?

No one wakes up in the morning saying, *"Today, I am going to behave and act in ways that exhaust my energy, and I'm going to do whatever I can to drain the energy of everyone I come in contact with."*

Sounds absurd, doesn't it? And yet, that is the net effect of what happens day in and day out in homes and offices everywhere—people living and working with their energy and their enthusiasm drained and exhausted, having performed at less than optimal levels. This is an impact of clarity amnesia.

However, at some point, triggered by an illness, perhaps, or a loss or other personal crisis—even just a vague sense of dissatisfaction—something stirs within clarity amnesiacs. They become seekers on a journey to recover what they've forgotten. Clues appear; but they can be baffled about which ones to follow. Then they begin to notice following some clues seems to *energize* them, while following others *exhausts* them. As they pursue more of the energizing clues, their curiosity quickens. It's at this point we see the process of remembering speed up; they feel vibrant and alive. The spell of amnesia is broken, and a vision of how they want to live their life unfolds before them.

Nurturing this newly restored or created vision and taking it into action is what *Get Clarity* is about. It offers a guided remedy for clarity amnesia—a step-by-step solution to aimless wandering that will lead you on an accelerated journey to a fulfilling life of peak experiences.

Separately and together, we've spent the past 25 years guiding people in aligning themselves with their purpose and direction. Even though many of our clients have come to us for help with something specific—discovering what's next in their lives, becoming better leaders, changing careers, perhaps, or finding their soul mate, we find as often as not they're in search of something larger and more enduring—living a lights-on life.

What does it look like to live "lights-on"?

- **Lights-on living means** when you wake up in the morning you know you will be doing work you love.

- **Lights-on living means** every day your relationships flow with give and take and are vibrant, energetic and filled with grace and ease.

- **Lights-on living means** you are conscious and aware—in every moment, of following your energy so you can live each day fully.

- **Lights-on living means** you have the ability to see when your thoughts and behaviors are not working and to shift your attention to be more effective. It's living with passion, purpose, and deeply connected action.

> **Practically speaking, living lights-on means following your own energetic signals, moving toward what inspires and revitalizes you—what "lights you up"—and away from what drains and demoralizes you. Energy, in this sense, is the invisible force that animates life; some call it chi, ki, prana, or élan vital.**

Although energy itself is invisible to the naked eye, its effect on the human system is obvious. Lights-on is a twinkle in the eye, a spring in the step, a glow around someone. Have you ever met someone who felt so alive, magnetic, and full of purpose their energy was almost contagious?

Lights-off is equally apparent: dull eyes, drooping posture, a listless dragging through life. And you don't just live in your own, individual energy bubbles; you're part of a vibrating, pulsating, electric, energetic world—a biofield; a matrix of all the different energies of the people and natural forces around you.

One of our clients, Daniel, tells us learning to live lights-on saved his marriage. Prior to learning how to read and follow energy, he had been frustrated with his wife, and for years had suffered a chronic discontent which naturally took a toll on their relationship.

He constantly thought of leaving. But with his focus always on the idea of ending things, he didn't focus on what made his marriage great. When he began to concentrate on what truly energized him, his perception of his marriage changed. Learning to discern his own energy is what saved his relationship, and his marriage.

Being in the flow

Living lights-on means literally *"going with the flow"*—the energetic flow of the universe and your own life. It comes from honoring the process of life and the energetic feedback from your surroundings and your own physiology. Learning to discern whether people, places, or events are energizing or draining will quickly become second nature. We call this *"cellular learning,"* because it happens at a visceral level: energy is experienced as a shift or feeling in the body. Your lights-on or lights-off response to daily happenings acts as an internal GPS—an energetic global positioning system to keep you on course living a life with clarity.

The *Get Clarity Operating System* we teach our clients is grounded in making choices on an energetic level: *taking apart the jigsaw puzzle of your life and seeing which pieces have energy in them—which light you up—then reassembling them in a configuration invested with more vibrancy and passion.* A vision, as we define it, is that cluster of lights-on clues.

The *Get Clarity* Partnership Journey Map

Every relationship follows a predictable pattern, whether they are long-term relationships or not. The flow is the same. There will always be a beginning, middle, and an end. Everything in life is constantly moving forward; and people with a positive edge on life have a system and get intentional about using *"flow patterns"*.

When most of our clients realize we've outlined this flow for them, it gives them a sense of confidence. It's like they've suddenly been given the keys to something they've just been guessing at for most of their lives! Many people continually react as if relationships are happening *to them*, and whatever comes next is a complete surprise. With this map of the river instead of wondering, feeling disoriented, and feeling *"lost in space"* they can visually see where they are on their journey. And every single one of them has also been able to pinpoint where they are on the map.

We use the map image of sailing down a river as the metaphor and flow pattern for the journey to lights-on life and fulfilling relationships. Since it's an action-oriented system, the map offers useful guidance and feedback as to where you are on your journey, how to move out of difficulties, and what you can look forward to. This map gives you action items in each step so you can move forward with greater ease, and stop circling around in less effective, draining actions.

For years, as Cathy worked with clients, the river image kept appearing to her as they talked about their life and their visioning process. She could visualize where a person was on the river and where he or she needed to go next.

The image was so strong that eventually Cathy drew a rough sketch of a river on a long piece of paper stretched around the walls of her office, and marked on it the twists and turns, setbacks, and challenges that her clients encountered. As Cathy drew this map, it became clear that it represented a universal journey that all clients experienced. Clear patterns emerged, and clients began using the map to help them plot the next leg of their journey. With the map—and their energetic GPS for guidance— they could navigate rapids and ride out storms as readily as they sailed over calm waters.

As with any journey it is helpful to have a map leading you to your destination. The *Get Clarity Partnership Journey Map* is available for you at this link—The book and the map are designed to work together, with the stations along the river corresponding to concepts outlined in the book. The link is: http:www.getclarity.com/partnership-map/. Password: getclarity. Many people like to post the map where they can refer to it throughout their journey.

> **When setting out on any journey, it is helpful to have a map leading you to your destination. The *Get Clarity Journey Map* is located in the back of this book. Where you can envision your own "lights-on" voyage. Both are designed to work together, with the stations along the river corresponding to concepts outlined in *Get Clarity* that can be referred to throughout your journey.**

How to Use This Book

Get Clarity for Powerful Partnering is divided into five parts, each covering a different stage on the lights-on journey.

Part I: Preparing for Departure introduces you to the visioning concept and outlines the fundamentals of energy, which is the foundation of our work. **Chapter One: Understanding Energy** explains energy fields and energy patterns in detail. **Chapter Two: Holding Your Own Energy Field** shows you how to retain you own energy under all circumstances—a critical step in staying aligned with your vision and keeping your relationships healthy. **Chapter Three: Looking for Lights-On** gives you an understanding of how energy manifests itself in the human system. **Chapter Four: Using Your Whole Brain** highlights the effect your thoughts have on your physiology.

Part II: Setting Your Course covers the essential work of defining your vision and removing obstacles—internal and external—to moving toward it.

By **Part III: Casting Off,** you're no longer at your mooring, in preparation mode, but sailing in open water. Here you will experience the power of intention in creating reality; you will explore the push-pull of attraction and resistance in following guidance. You will also learn how to fine-tune your vision and align it with effective action, as well as how to navigate difficult choice points without being paralyzed with indecision.

Part IV: Correcting Course guides you through those rough waters—the inevitable challenges and setbacks any visioning journey and relationship encounter. There is advice on recognizing when to push forward and when to drop anchor and stay still.

Part V: Sailing Home brings the visioning process to fruition. Here, you will discover the magic of synchronicity and the importance of living in the present moment. You will also learn when it's advisable to adopt a Plan B. You will get a taste of the *"whoosh effect"*—the exhilarating acceleration that occurs near the end of the vision journey, speeding you to your goal. We end with a recap of the inner transformation that signals a lights-on life.

In the **Appendix,** we give guidance on what to do Post Partnership to stay committed to a greater vision that serves both parties.

Since some of the terms we use in our work may be unfamiliar, we've also included a **Glossary** that supplements the definitions provided in the text.

Each chapter offers insights and strategies to reconnect you with your passion and vision and expand with the co-creative energy of a partner. At the end of each chapter are two summary sections to aid you in your journey. **Clarity in Action** contains real-life stories of people who have used these tools to create a new reality and new relationships for themselves.

In **Navigational Tools**, we suggest specific steps to help you move toward your goal.

Taken together, the strategies, steps, and personal stories in this book are designed to help you:

- Discover what lights you up and what's next in your life, and how to co-create with a partner.

- Attract what you want and release what you don't want.

- Create powerful relationships energetically.

- Recognize choice points and use them to create your optimum reality.

- Understand *"shadow behavior"* so it won't become a divisive pattern in your partnership.

- Eliminate self-criticism, judgment, blame, jealousy, compromise, and other debilitating patterns.

- Find the lessons—and silver lining—in detours and setbacks.

- Learn the power of synergy, which allows you both to magnify your individual energy exponentially.

Our culture seems to endorse struggle and effort as the most effective means to achieve success. It continually reinforces messages like *"Life is hard"* and *"Do it even if it kills you."* Or *"No pain no gain."* But this is not the true path to success: diligence is one thing, but excessive negative stress and pressure lead only to exhaustion.

We propose an alternative—a *"loving what you do and doing what you love"* lifestyle and a lights-on approach to all of your relationships.

It begins with an inspired vision of what you want your life to look like; that's merged with a co-created shared vision of partnership with your partner, and the shared vision draws on both of your lights-on energy to achieve it. Passion and enthusiasm will help you create your visions, individually and together. And having a clear vision to hold on to will keep you from getting knocked out of the game by others' well-intended opinions and advice, or your own doubts and fears.

The system and practices in this book are all time-tested by our workshops and individual coaching. We've found people who've awakened to their destiny and are living a lights-on life invariably report the

same thing: regardless of the obstacles they encountered, they never lost sight of their individual vision
in the context of a shared partnership vision.

They simply adjusted their strategy, timing, or
financing until they both were able to see their
dream come true.

In the pages that follow you'll find the tools and
encouragement you need to overcome obstacles and
complete your visioning journey, guided by the
lights-on wisdom of your heart, and the synergy of
partnership.

Chapter One
Understanding Energy

*No doubt you can think of people you know
who seem to radiate stronger energy than others,
as if their energy field is somehow bigger or more potent.*
—William Collinge, Author

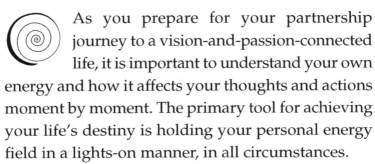 As you prepare for your partnership journey to a vision-and-passion-connected life, it is important to understand your own energy and how it affects your thoughts and actions moment by moment. The primary tool for achieving your life's destiny is holding your personal energy field in a lights-on manner, in all circumstances.

You were born with a personal GPS, or inner guidance system—an instinctive knowing of what energizes you and what drains you. The concepts and tools set out in the following chapters are focused on helping you learn to use your personal GPS, so you can control your own energy at all times.

There are several important facts about energy to help you in this regard:

- Your body is a biological energy field that interacts constantly with the environment, creating a feedback loop.

- If you interpret this feedback as stressful, the result will be a loss of your vital energy and you will feel negative, drained, and lights-off.

- If you interpret the feedback as exciting, the result will be an increase in your vital energy, and you will feel positive, energized, and lights-on.

- The interpretation of the energy feedback in your life is your job. No one else's energy is your responsibility. You cannot manage your own energy and the energy of all the people in your life; it's just not possible.

Holding your own personal energy steadily and not letting yourself become drained or frenetic is the key to creating a vibrant life. To help maintain your positive energy in all you do, recognize there are three distinct energy fields you are in touch with at all times.

The Three Energy Fields

Your Personal Field:
The Human Energy System

Your personal energy field is the arm's-length space around you, like an invisible energy bubble. It contains your mind and your thoughts, your body, your health, your spirit and your creativity.

You control your personal energy field through the moment-to-moment choices you make. By choosing what you think, how you nourish or deplete your body, how you exercise, and how you sleep, as well as how you enliven your spirit, you can stay energetically alive, conscious, and lights-on.

The language you use helps create your reality, so it's important to use positive talk and speak in a way that accurately describes the energy you are sensing in yourself and in the people, places, and situations around you.

Avoid statements like:

> *"It kills me to hear that." Or "I'm so angry at
> /afraid of what's happening in the world."*

The simple practice of speaking an energetic language—*"that lights me up,"* or *"that knocks my lights out"*— will shift your focus, making you more aware of the energy around you, and will enable you to make better choices.

The Near Field:
The Environmental Energy System

The near field is the energy your personal energy field interacts with daily, in your immediate environment—your home, your family, your neighborhood, your office, and your community. The near field is your support field. This is the field of partnership.

Although you have less control over this field than over your personal energy field, your thoughts and actions have a strong influence on it. Influence is the key word here; you cannot control anyone else's field but your actions and behaviors will absolutely influence it.

You interact with your near field constantly, so it is critical you do all you can to ensure its impact on you is supportive and enlivening. You can best affect this field in a positive way by choosing your friends, partners, and immediate surroundings with intention and care.

To keep your personal energy alive in the near field, ask yourself:

> *"Does my environment enhance my life?" "Do I feel soothed when I walk into my home or office?"*
> *"Do my friends, partners, and neighbors support me? Are my relationships loving and kind?"*

If the answer to any of these questions is *"no"*, take the action necessary to change it, whether it's de-cluttering your home, or letting go of friends who are energy drains. (In later chapters, we'll suggest specific action in this area.)

The Remote Field:
The Distant Energy System

The remote energy field is the one most distant from you. This is the energy of systems and events in the larger world over which you have little or no control—war, the economy, social upheaval, and natural disasters.

Even if you are not directly involved in these areas, you are impacted by their energy. From the time you were very young, the culture tended to direct your focus to events in the remote field. Think of the subjects you studied at school: history, geography, international relations, the social and physical sciences. The daily news bombards us with information about wars and conflicts, the ups and downs of the economy, crime, natural catastrophes, and global tragedies.

> **When you let negativity in this field consume you, and you worry about events you cannot control, you can easily lose your own energy, becoming anxious and on edge.**

To keep your energy alive when you relate to events in the remote field, reduce your exposure to the news media. Try going to bed without watching the late-night news, then notice if your sleep is more restful and you wake up with less anxiety. Listen to positive talk radio and other media outlets delivering news without using sensationalized stories, fear based "hooks", alarmist language, or harsh voice tones.

Tune in to positive messages and read publications offering balanced coverage. This isn't to suggest you ignore what's going on in the world, but rather choose carefully how you receive the news, as a way to keep from being consumed by energy-draining negativity.

Calibrating Your Energy

Humans are hard-wired to look for light. Our earliest ancestors survived by quickly reading the energy signals of people and the environment. They would scan the horizon for areas of dark—signs of danger to be avoided—and areas of light, which indicated what was safe to approach. You still use this ancient communication system to answer the question, *"Is there anything unsafe or wrong here?"* In every new situation you automatically scan the environment to decide whether to approach or avoid. Once safety is assured, you move forward.

This same energetic scan ability is the skill you will use as your primary guide to making light-on choices for yourself. To make it easier to calibrate the energy in your personal field, we developed a simple tool—the energy meter—allowing you to assess the effect of your interactions on your vital life force—both external and internal.

Any interaction with a person, place, or event generates an energy exchange. The energy meter enables you to guide your choices in the direction of more energy for yourself.

The Energy Meter

The meter registers three basic types of energetic exchange:

- Draining: You feel tired and worn out when the interaction is finished.

- Energizing: You feel more alive and awake when the interaction is finished.

- Neutral: The interaction has no impact on your energy.

Neutral

Lights-Off   **Lights-On**
Drained   **Energized**

At the low end of the meter, stagnant or lights-off energy is experienced as confusion, limits, mindless action, drama, and depleted energy.

At the high end of the meter, lights-on energy, or "flow," is experienced as clarity, intentional action, a sense of possibility, and vibrant energy. Although it's arbitrary, in our experience, choices that calibrate at 7.5 and above are very clearly lights-on.

Using the energy meter as a mental reference point, you can gauge what will happen when your energy field comes into contact with other energy fields, so you can make choices allowing you to do more of what energizes you and less of what drains you.

Energy Patterns

Energy is an invisible force only recognizable by sensing or observing the effects or results of its presence. Energy in the human body is recognizable in the patterns driving your behavior. To journey through life *"in flow,"* you need to understand which energy patterns drain you and slow you down or stop you.

Quickly recognizing draining energy patterns is what we call **rapid discovery**; using strategies to speedily return to energizing thoughts and actions is what we call **rapid recovery**.

Patterns are discernible in your own personal field and the fields of those around you.

Just as a sailor uses knowledge of the constellations in the night sky to plot a course, recognizing the patterns in your personal field will make it easier for you to navigate while on your Clarity journey. Energy patterns tend to operate unconsciously; so to create flow in your life it is critical that you bring these patterns to conscious awareness.

Of the many different energy patterns in existence, there are two especially useful to understand, because they have such a strong effect on the ability to live lights-on. These patterns are light and shadow, and monkey mind.

Light and Shadow

Light patterns are those energizing you and getting you into flow; such as *trust, self-esteem, generosity, innocence, curiosity, faith, vision, enthusiasm, co-operation, innovation, perfection, manifestation, playfulness, and service.*

Shadow patterns are energy patterns that stop you, *such as fear, doubt, obligation, self-pity, anxiety, guilt, envy, competition, compromise, attachment, martyrdom, and imitation.*

The more clarity you have about both your light and shadow patterns, the easier it will be to recognize when your shadow has stepped in to sabotage you. The shadow is always present.

The psychiatrist Carl Jung wrote:

Everyone carries a shadow, and the less it is embodied in the individual's conscious life, the blacker and denser it is.

Failure to recognize your *"dark side"* is a major block to realizing your full potential. However, when you focus on the light—on what energizes you—the shadow does lose its power.

People who successfully manifest their vision will first recognize their shadow behavior—rapid discovery. Then they are able to move past it by switching their focus and going into action with behavior lighting them up—rapid recovery. The premise is simple: if you follow your light you will get more light—you will feel more energized.

Monkey Mind

Monkey mind is a Buddhist concept that refers to the tendency of the mind to jump around like a drunken monkey, especially when you're trying to be calm. Put another way, monkey mind refers to the constant internal chattering in your head.

On the *Get Clarity* journey, we have a slightly different interpretation of monkey mind. To us, it's the critical, self-protective voice warning you of danger.

In this sense, monkey mind has its origins in the fight-or-flight syndrome. This primitive alert system in the body interprets change of any sort as dangerous. The constant change in today's world sends a change=danger signal to the adrenal system, putting the body on high alert.

As the stress hormone cortisol builds up, it produces energy patterns of doubt, worry, anxiety, restlessness, fatigue, disturbed sleep, inability to focus, alienation, and hopelessness.

The most noticeable result of monkey mind chatter is it distracting you from the present moment. Here's an example: Suppose you're lunching with a friend, engaged in a lights-on conversation. Your brain is interested and alert. Then all of a sudden starts chattering about some trivial matter or judgment. While your friend is sharing something heartfelt, your monkey mind is criticizing the wardrobe choice of a woman across the room. You're still seated at the table, but you're not fully present. Monkey mind's internal monologue has taken charge of the situation.

After many hours of conversation with our coaching clients, we've observed some common patterns of expression that all monkey mind conversations seem to share. While this is not a scientific study, our observations are useful, and they add humor to a deeper understanding of this energy pattern.

- Monkey mind speaks constantly and is rarely quiet.

- Monkey mind has the speech sophistication and sentence structure of a five-year-old child.

- The monkey mind speech pattern is repetitive, saying the same things over and over, like a tape loop running incessantly in the brain.

- The content of monkey mind speech is overwhelmingly negative, laden with worst-case scenarios.

This constant din is a universal problem, and there are a number of meditative practices aimed at quieting the mind. However, even dedicated practitioners often have difficulty achieving a calm mental state for more than a few minutes at a time. So, if the pros find it hard to turn off monkey mind, how are we ordinary mortals supposed to override those tapes in our head?

Fortunately, we've found a way. Whenever our clients get stuck in monkey mind, we coach them to recognize and acknowledge the chatter, then shift their attention over to what lights them up.

The technique we use is simple: Instead of resisting monkey mind, address it directly by turning to your right and saying, *"Thank you for sharing."*

Then, turn to your left and consciously switch your focus to a positive, lights-on action. You could, for example, do a check-in like the one described in the next chapter, or work with your vision map—a graphic presentation of your *Get Clarity* journey that you'll learn more about in Chapter Seven: Designing Your Vision.

Another effective recovery strategy is to find a relaxation practice appealing to you enough to practice it regularly. Engage in some sort of mind-body practice, which can include prayer, yoga, deep breathing, and meditation to hypnosis, guided imagery, and labyrinth walking.

The brain responds to input either in our environment or what we provide through our thoughts and pictures (the language of the brain).

If it's not getting different external input from our environment like a walk, listening to music, or any of the above examples to shift out of the monkey mind, we can shift the internal input. Create positive mantras, new pictures based on positive outcomes, or wishes. One of our favorite mantras we hand out to clients is a visual reminder that reflects on their windshield, *"Things are always working out for me."*

Chapter Two

Holding Your Own Energy Field

The antidote to exhaustion is not rest...
the antidote to exhaustion is wholeheartedness.
—David Whyte, Author and Poet

Life today exposes us to more drama—and melodrama—than ever before, especially in the media. It's easy to fall into the trap of confusing drama with energy. The key distinction between the two: drama is draining, while energy is enlivening.

To avoid being drained, focus on holding your own energy during all interactions. *Learning how to consistently hold your own personal energy field is the most important element of creating the life you want to live.*

As you develop this critical skill, you will notice your personal field becoming steadier and stronger. With experience you will seldom feel drained, and the *"energy vampires"* will have to go elsewhere for their juice.

There are two key strategies to assist you in developing and sustaining—holding—a strong and intentional personal field—the *daily check-in* and the *daily personal ritual*.

Daily Check-In

The daily check-in is one of the most important tools to keep you in energetic and conscious flow. It consists of asking yourself a series of questions and paying attention to your answers. The time of day when you do your check-in is up to you, but if you do it first thing in the morning, you can start off the day with a clean slate. On the other hand, doing your check-in at night is a good way to clear away the residue of the day and set your intention for tomorrow.

You can do the check-in on your own, or with someone else. When done alone, the check-in is an internal conversation that will ground you and keep you focused. When done with another person, it becomes a very powerful relationship tool that deepens the connection between you and improves communication and understanding. But whether you do the check-in alone or with another person, remember the primary purpose is to focus on yourself and on holding your own energy field against the pressures of your monkey mind and the energy drain from others in your near field. If you're doing the check-in with someone else, be sure to effectively listen to one another and refrain from commenting on or criticizing what the other person says.

The five questions to ask yourself in the daily check-in are:

1. *What's different?*

2. *What worked and what didn't work?*

3. *What is the state of my mind, body, and spirit?*

4. *What am I grateful for?*

5. *What is my intention for today?*

What's different?

One of the principles of quantum physics is that every nanosecond, everything changes. Noticing differences—what has changed, whether in your thinking or your surroundings— keeps you open to possibilities. Asking yourself, *"What's different?"* is a simple way to stay alert and avoid operating from old patterns.

The answer to *"What's different?"* doesn't have to be profound. Even a mundane answer like, *"It's sunny today"* or, *"I feel tired"* will shake you out of a world-weary, *"same old, same old"* mentality. The simple mechanism of asking the question helps you access a place of conscious awareness.

What worked and what didn't work?

Review your performance over the past twenty-four hours, then ask yourself *what worked* and *what didn't work*. Comment only on your own performance, not on what others have or haven't done, even if they were key players in the experience. This is very important. The intention of this part of the check-in is to remove all forms of judgment and criticism from your personal field.

This non-judgmental, facts-only evaluation of your performance is similar to what athletes do when they watch films of past games to see where they could improve. Be sure to give equal time to what worked and what didn't work. If you focus more on what didn't work, judgment and criticism are bound to creep in.

You're simply looking for information. Another way of asking what didn't work might be, *"What in my thoughts and actions could I have done differently to be more effective?"* If you begin to see patterns in what didn't work, you can develop strategies to change your performance. If you see you frequently inter-rupt people, for example, you can set the intention to become more aware and stop this behavior.

Another step in this part of the daily check-in is to acknowledge your responses by clapping your hands to applaud yourself. This may seem trivial or silly, but it's very important to celebrate your answers, and celebrate them all equally. You're not really applauding the answers per se but rather your willingness to take an honest look at your performance and acknowledge what you discover.

What is the state of my mind, body, and spirit?

The intention of this part of the check-in is for you to live in distinction—to be able to assess your energy and make choices from that perspective—by seeing a clear separation between your mind, body, and spirit. It is common to describe your personal field as if only one of those three areas was affected. For example, you might say to yourself, *"I woke up with a backache, and now my whole day is ruined."*

However, a check-in might reveal that yes, your body aches, but your mind is busy and alert, and your spirit is light and energized. Hardly a prescription for a ruined day.

It's also important to note your spirit is always described positively. Words like happy, joyful, expansive, light, soaring, calm, peaceful, and creative most aptly describe it.

What am I grateful for?

Much has been written about the value of focusing on the positive in your life. Research has shown people who express gratitude on a frequent basis are more optimistic, feel better about their lives, are more energetic and alert, and make more progress towards their goals. In addition to feeling better, new studies show gratitude can change our bio-chemistry and release positive neurochemicals.

By answering *"What am I grateful for?"* each day, you shift your attention to what you have, rather than what you don't have. This focus allows you to approach your day with more vitality.

What is my intention for today?

An intention is different from an affirmation. While an affirmation is a positive statement, such as *"I am worthy of money,"* an intention focuses on action: *"My intention today is to generate money flow, make six sales calls, and have fun doing it."*

The power of intention in achieving goals has been well documented. Manifesting what you want in your life begins with setting an intention, then taking action towards it.

Daily Personal Ritual

A personal ritual that you perform every day is the second essential tool for holding your energy. A ritual can ground you, connect you to your intentions, and anchor your approach to your daily interactions. When you use your personal ritual, you are choosing to live with clarity and compassion.

The ritual can help you disengage from any drama in a situation, so you become an observer rather than an absorber. Like a mirror you can simply reflect back the drama energy coming at you, rather than soaking it up like a sponge. Your personal ritual sets your personal energy field.

Personal rituals can take many forms. Some of our clients walk first thing in the morning; some do a meditation before they leave their beds, or before they fall asleep at night. The key is to make the ritual a habit, one you'll remember to do at certain times. The brain loves time-based habits; it takes much less willpower or brain created power to "make" you do it.

We prefer a verbal ritual—an invocation focused on bringing positive energy into your personal field. You can create your own ritual by starting with the qualities you want in your personal field—peace, beauty, love, and the like. Make the ritual simple and easy to repeat either to yourself or aloud.

Here is one example:

God, Universe, and all other Guides, grant me wisdom, skill, and knowledge to be of highest service to all. Assist me in holding a constant energy field around me at all times so I feel only love and see only beauty. Let this force field attract others so I may attract love, joy, connection, community, and abundance.

You may find it helpful to ground yourself before you begin your ritual. Close your eyes and visualize dropping an imaginary cord down to the center of the earth. With both feet firmly on the ground, breathe deeply and feel the connection you have with the earth.

If you wish, you can use a mudra or hand gesture. Mudra is a Sanskrit word meaning "seal" or "sign" referrring to the ritual hand gestures many yogis use during meditation practice. Other traditions also use hand gestures. For example, Christians put palms together while praying, and Qigong masters turn their palms to the heavens to call in universal energy. Any higher quality you aspire to can be sealed and activated with its own mudra.

> **It is very important that your daily ritual be done in a conscious manner.**
> Be aware of the words as you repeat them: feel them in your body; sense how they impact you. When you say, *"I feel only love,"* or *"I attract joy,"* let the feeling of love flow through your body and let the joy be expressed in your face, your smile. Most important, let your ritual serve you by reconnecting you to the sacred aspects of your life and setting your energy for the day.

As we've said, holding your own personal energy field is the most important step in achieving your destiny. The practice of performing a daily check-in and a daily personal ritual will help you stay aware, conscious, and focused on your vision.

Chapter Three
Looking for Lights-On

All that is in the heart is written in the face.
—African proverb

Looking for lights-on is a new way of seeing, and once you learn this skill, it will profoundly enhance all of your communications. Seeing what lights people up is an innovative approach to living—heightening your innate ability to tune into the energetic signals and vitality cues constantly being sent and received in the world around you. Learning to conduct a quick and accurate visual scan to identify levels of passion and energy in yourself and others is a fundamental skill for living energetically.

From the beginning, we have used camera feedback in our work so our clients can see the physical changes appear in their face as a result of focusing their thoughts and actions on the things energizing them. This photographic feedback is evidence of the power of their own energy, helping them deepen their understanding of what they can achieve.

> (◎) Lights-on is easy to see, once you get used to what we call **high noticing**— reading energetic signals and vitality clues. When you light up, not only do you feel the energy in your body but your exterior physiology will also look different to others. High noticing applies whether you are seeing another person's physiology or seeing & sensing your own.

The following looking-for-lights tutorial consists of four pairs of photos, taken before and after an "energetic" interview—an interview where we track a person's lights-on energy. The photos—each pair was taken in a professional setting under identical lighting conditions—demonstrate the physical transformation occurring after the people discussed their most expansive visions with a coach for between 60 and 120 minutes. *The differences in the before and after photos are striking.*

But even under ordinary conditions, you can see the same lights-on qualities in someone's face: balance, vitality, connection, and luminosity. In everyday interactions, people's faces shift rapidly, and your eye will notice the physiology changing from moment to moment.

In the first three pairs of photos, the physical changes were solely the result of a lights-on focus of thoughts. None of these people had yet taken any action toward fulfilling their lights-on dreams.

Increased light in eyes
Increased focus
More present and connected

Balanced light in both eyes
Right and left sides of
face balanced
More integrated overall

Increased focus and clarity
More present and energized
More relaxed and integrated

The following photos show what happens when lights-on thoughts are followed by aligned action. Here, six months elapsed between the before and after shots. They show the deeper, more sustainable physical change that comes with living lights-on.

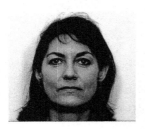 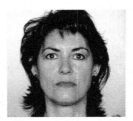

More luminosity overall
More approachable
More direct focus

Photographs used with the permission of the subjects

The changes you see in the preceding photos are a result of the body's ability to make an energetic shift internally, and then feedback those changes where they can be seen and felt externally. When you are tuned in to energetic clues and can communicate by responding to the energy of others, your interactions will be more vibrant and connected.

Pausing a moment to notice other 's lights-on/ lights-off energy is far more effective than living on autopilot. In Powerful Partnering, this is called high noticing and is imperative for communication between partners. And calibrating your own energy by sensing your own lights-on level will enable you to redirect your focus and navigate choice points—dilemmas, transitions, logjams in the river—with certainty. You will have the power and knowledge to choose an energized future by following your lights.

Chapter Four
Using Your Whole Brain

Brain: an apparatus with which we think we think.
—Ambrose Bierce, Author

Your thoughts create your reality: Change your thinking, change your life. This sentence is a mantra for many of us, but what does it really mean? In the *Get Clarity* journey it also means that your thoughts can change your physiology; your cellular lights-on state; and your whole brain response. Which, in turn, changes your reality.

When you switch from a stressed-out, depleted, lights-off state to a calm, energized, lights-on state, it creates a sequence of physical changes in your system. You reflect, look, feel, act, and attract differently. Here's what we mean:

- **Reflect:** Lights-on energy emits a noticeable radiance and vitality—an inner glow. Lights-on is an inside job.

- **Look:** Lights-on energy has an overall balanced, lighter, more uplifted appearance.

- **Feel:** Lights-on energy is sensed as vital and timeless. It embodies flow with grace and ease. It is effortless.

- **Act:** Lights-on actions are purposeful and aligned with your vision. They're focused on doing more of what energizes you and less of what drains you. Before you act, you should ask the all-important questions: *What do I want right now? What will it take to make it happen?*

- **Attract:** Lights-on energy is attractive. The energy you send out is the energy you attract: Like attracts like. In high-energy exchanges, lights-on energy creates the magic.

What directions are you giving this vehicle, your body? Your answer is the essence of the *Get Clarity* journey. You are meant to live a balanced and energized life. And it all starts with your thoughts. Taking a vision into action requires whole brain thinking.

> (◎) Whole brain thinking creates systems and outcomes from a balanced communication between right brain (EQ—chaos) and left brain (IQ—order). Think of it as having a 360° awareness and meta-cognition. A whole brain flow pattern has the right and left hemispheres communicating and integrating information in a balanced fashion. The integration of these two dominant thought patterns lays the foundation for a balanced viewpoint which we define as **global intelligence** (GQ).

Basic brain anatomy divides the brain into two symmetrical regions, a right hemisphere and a left hemisphere, connected by a thick bundle of some 300 million nerve fibers called the corpus callosum, which passes information between the hemispheres.

The right brain has been termed the emotional intelligence (EQ) center. Dreaming, diffuse thinking or chaos works from this hemisphere of your brain.

This hemisphere of the brain reasons holistically, uses metaphors, sees pictures simultaneously, recognizes patterns, and interprets emotions and nonverbal expressions. Well-developed emotional intelligence is an accurate predictor of performance in a relationship setting.

The left brain is where intelligence quotient (IQ) resides. Linear thinking, planning and order work from this hemisphere.

This hemisphere of the brain reasons logically, rarely uses metaphors, sees words in sequence, excels at analysis, and handles language. A well-developed IQ is an accurate predictor of performance in an academic setting.

Here's how it works in your body. At the cellular level, when there is a balanced communication between the hemispheres, a cascade of hormonal events occurs and as you have seen in the previous chapter, the most noticeable effect is a type of radiance in the forehead and a twinkle in the eye, which we call lights-on.

This lights-on response to integrated brain functioning occurs at the site of the pineal gland, which sits in the center of the brain, between the two hemispheres.

Scientists now know the pineal gland is sensitive to light from external sources like night and day. (A lack of external light is implicated in depression and seasonal attitudinal depression disorder.) The pineal gland is also sensitive to light from internal sources due to the increase of or decrease of serotonin. For centuries ancient texts and mystical writings have called this pineal function a "third eye." This third eye response of lighting up reflects an integration of the two sides of the brain and it is associated with insight, or you might say, the mind's eye.

When global intelligence shows up in your physical body as lights-on, it sets the field for creative solutions and sustainable outcomes to be created.

This whole brain way of thinking is an integrated communication system, a feedback loop. It is the key driver that keeps a vivid vision operating in concert with a strategic & tactical plan. The process then requires translation, through clear communication, into aligned systems and performance to make it a reality.

Using the skill of high noticing focuses your attention, and focused attention is the physical force, which shapes the neural pathways of the brain. The lights-on response trains your brain to become the participatory observer—thus creating new neural pathways, which maintain and stabilize this learned brain state.

This global intelligence is a unified perceptual field of intelligence that is creative, insightful, and enables you to grasp the overall context linking component parts and binds them with meaning. This perception helps you to reframe your experience and transforms your understanding of it, which creates a wisdom perspective.

The wisdom perspective and resultant, newly created, neural pathways allow you to make more effective, high-value choices. When you communicate from a lights-on and balanced perspective, the translation results in coherent information. This information directs performance into an alignment with the whole perspective.

Review the qualities of EQ, IQ and GQ below:

Review the qualities of EQ, IQ and GQ below:

Right hemisphere (EQ)	Left hemisphere (IQ)	Whole/global brain (GQ)
Movement on left side of body	Movement on right side of body	
Visual/spatial	Verbal	
Nonlinear	Linear	
Dreaming/what	Planning/how-to	Grasps overall context
Diffuse thinking/ chaos	Focal thinking/order	Cognitively reframes experience
Excels at intuition	Excels at analysis	Excels at linking component parts
Reasons simultaneously	Reasons sequentially	Binds component parts w/meaning
Sees patterns/ relationships	Sees sequence of concepts	Sees as an impartial observer
Sees pictures simultaneously	Sees words in orderly progression	Uses 360° seeing/ meta-awareness

PART II

Set Your Course

Chapter Five

Planning Your Journey

*There is a vitality, a life-force, an energy, a quickening that
is translated through you into action, and because
there is only one of you in all of time, this expression is
unique and if you block it, it will never exist through
any medium and will be lost…the world will not have it.
It is not your business to determine how good it is,
nor how valuable, nor how it compares with other
expressions…it is your business to keep it yours,
clearly and directly, to keep the channel open.*
—Martha Graham, Dancer, Choreographer

Before we begin any journey—say, a long-planned vacation—we're filled with anticipation, excited at the prospect of having a wonderful adventure and open to the possibilities of what may happen. This juiced-up, energizing sense of anticipation is a wonderful part of the whole experience.

The same is true of the *Get Clarity* journey. Your enthusiasm for what you are beginning will generate energy that will propel you to the next step of your journey. When you allow yourself to dream, and to be truly open to the possibilities for your life, you create a flow of energy throughout your body. You can feel it. And as you saw in the photos in Chapter Three, you look different, too. What's more, you act and attract in a different way. You are using your whole brain to create your vision and you know at the deepest level of your being that anything is possible.

One key aspect of starting your *Clarity* journey is giving yourself permission to have everything you want and to live each day vibrantly and passionately.

Many people do not allow themselves the time and space to dream about what they want. As you begin your own search for what's next, you will discover that taking the time to experience your biggest and most passionate dreams will release a burst of energetic flow.

In a past *Get Clarity* workshop we gave the participants a brief visioning exercise in which they shared with someone their dream for one small aspect of their life. In the discussion that ensued, one of the participants articulated a reaction we've heard many times:

> *In just ten minutes of allowing myself to express what I truly want to another person, I felt more*

alive than I have in a very long time. Merely talking about it gives me incredible energy. I want to keep it going.

This burst of aliveness and energy is what we want you to experience in this first stage of your journey. Dreaming is a critical, energizing beginning to putting a life-affirming vision into action.

What is a Vision?

Webster's dictionary defines a vision as *"a mental image; especially an imaginative contemplation."*

For the purpose of your *Get Clarity* journey, a vision is a collection of what we call lights-on clues—thoughts about, and images of, a goal that deeply energizes you when contemplating it.

Your vision is a clear mental image creating a vital connection to unlimited possibilities for the future. Having a vivid picture of how you want your life to be generates energy at the core of your very being. As you develop this picture in detail, it will keep you passionately and relentlessly focused while you embark on making it real.

Much has been written about what it takes to be successful. One of the common denominators is successful people have a clear vision of what they want to achieve and a passionate desire to accomplish it. Imagine applying the same successful vision to your partnership; using the power and energy of two committed to a larger vision. In the *Get Clarity* journey, the vision we want you to create for yourself is a heart-connected image. A vision is more than just a good idea. It is a good idea rooted in your heart, your most passionate energy source.

Start Dreaming

To create a vision for your life and partnership driven by passionate energy, you have to exercise your right brain. Dreaming works from the right hemisphere. While the left-brain is linear in processing information, the right brain is holistic. It sees the big picture; the left-brain handles the details. The right brain is visual, dealing in images. Its mode of knowing is intuitive, while the logical left-brain sticks to the facts.

Allowing yourself to dream, to imagine, and to be fully open to your intuition gives your right brain full rein to do its work. Many of the tools you will learn in this book are aimed at awakening and engaging your right brain. (Don't worry: there is plenty for your left-brain to do on the journey: you'll need it for taking concrete action.)

Being aware of your energy and how it is impacted by your thoughts will help you engage your whole body in seeing, sensing, and using your energy to help you achieve your vision. So, dream big—let your most expansive vision guide you both, individually and together.

Clarity in Action: Ryan's Story

Ryan is a very successful cactus and plant grower. Before he was a teenager, he had a passion for the unique beauty of cactus and other succulents. Throughout high school and college his avocation was raising and mutating different variations of his plants.

Thirty years ago, after graduating with a PhD in Clinical Psychology, Ryan decided to take a year off before beginning a professional practice and spend the time doing what he loved most—growing cactus and succulents. He also truly loved working in partnership with his wife. His simple vision for the year was to be next to his wife every day, getting his hands dirty doing what he loved while creating an opportunity for others to appreciate having cacti in their home.

Ryan and his wife spent this first year growing cacti in their backyard and selling them out of his car trunk to nurseries in their area. As visions are prone to do, his grew into something else. Visions have a tendency to evolve and change when put into action. His initial vision led to a small leased acreage where he could expand his gardens, and expanded again to a vision of buying an even larger farm and significantly growing the operation.

Over time his vision became one of creating a much larger company selling varieties of cactus throughout the United States. Ryan's company now farms several hundred acres, employs a few hundred employees, and has revenue exceeding $70 million a year.

However, much of the original underlying and driving vision is still the same—*working with his wife and partner every day getting cacti into homes so people can appreciate the beauty of the plants.*

Navigational Tools: Start Dreaming

To begin the process of creating a vision, sit comfortably and allow a quiet space to open up in your mind. Imagine that you are in a place that gives you a sense of calm, such as sitting by a country spring flowing with fresh, clear water. Or maybe on a beach with the waves gently hitting the sand, or in a forest with fresh, clean air where you can hear birds chirping and feel a gentle breeze as the trees sway. Plan to spend at least sixty minutes dreaming and exploring the place within you where anything and everything is possible.

- In this quiet place, begin to envision the changes you want in your life. Let go of any limiting beliefs or negative ideas you are holding onto. Be radical and expansive: admit all possibilities.

- Start by asking yourself this question: In the field of all possibilities, *what do I want?* (We call this the "Santa Claus question"—pretend that you're Santa Claus and can give yourself anything you want. What would that be?)

- After you have opened your vision to this unlimited place, you ask yourself:
What do I want in my relationships?
What do I want in my professional and work life? What do I want in my personal life?

- Stay in the vision place of what you want to create and don't get sidetracked into thinking about how you will make it happen. Trust that all action steps will come in right timing after your vision is clear.

- As you finish answering the questions and emerge from the dreaming state, be prepared to write down everything you remember— every detail of what you envisioned, no matter how wild or crazy it seems. These wild and crazy thoughts are what we call *"lights-on clues."* As you move forward on your journey, these clues will be combined with other clues, connecting to form a clear picture of your vision. These clues will soon be used to synchronize with your partner's vision.

Refine Your Focus

When we are conducting visioning interviews with clients we ask them what they want, often the response is *"I want everything."* Unfortunately, wanting everything provides no clear and focused direction, and no specific action to achieve your desired outcome.

Cultivating curiosity is the first step to refining your focus, individually and as partners. Being curious and exploratory about what you both want opens you up to new ideas.

In visioning interviews each partner envisions their own individual ideas, then we pull together what they want as a couple. As empowered partners, it's important to co-create a powerful vision together, providing the necessary guidance toward what you want to bring into your lives.

Together you are more powerful and you will both need to refine your focus by gathering more lights-on clues.

You also become open to looking at new ways to follow your dreams; ways that weren't available to you before you began your visioning. Sometimes you get stuck in a rut based on cultural programming, the way it was done in your family, or how you believe things should look.

Einstein said: *"We can't solve problems by using the same kind of thinking we used when we created them.*

Becoming curious allows you to look at your visions in a new and unique way, one based in the kind of imaginative thinking used to create new ideas.

And being aware of whether these new ideas energize or drain you will guide you in making sure you're putting your attention on what lights you up.

> **Remember: Where you put your attention will refine your focus and ultimately create greater clarity. A clear focus will allow your initial dreamy vision to expand, and the resulting more expansive vision will show you in what direction to move.**

Remaining curious and paying attention to following your energy will also help you remain open to the unexpected. All kinds of wonderful mysteries and surprises await you on your journey together, but if you think you already know everything, you will fail to notice them.

The more you notice without the filter of your opinions and preconceptions, the more you will be shown. So stop analyzing and instead pay attention to what your energy and intuition are showing you. Refining your focus creates a refined, more expansive vision versus the aimless wandering which can come from wanting everything.

The bottom line in refining your vision is to follow what lights you up. Since your attention goes where your thoughts go, and your attention directs your focus, it's critically important you focus on *what you want* rather than *what is not working*.

Focusing on what lights you up is a far more energizing, enjoyable and effective way to spend your days. When you operate on a daily basis doing what energizes you and serves a passion-based vision, you attract more of what you want. Like attracts like.

Take action by pursuing more of the lights-on items on your list. Doing more of what lights you up will naturally point you in the direction of your vision. And, when you begin to focus on the people and things that light you up, your energy naturally increases.

Navigational Tools: Refine Your Focus

Refining your focus involves identifying whatever lights you up. Be an energy detective in your own life.

- Take a 24-hour period, and throughout the day, be fully aware, and observe everything you do and everyone you interact with.

- Ask yourself two questions during every interaction or action:
  Am I more alive, more energized, more lights-on?
  Am I duller, more drained, more lights-off?

- Keep notes throughout the day on which interactions energize you and which ones drain you.

- At the end of the 24 hours, list all your actions and interactions and rate each on a scale of 1 to 10 on the Energy Meter. Write down your ratings and note which items are lights-on. (Generally, anything above 7.5 is considered lights-on.)

Live in Distinction

Living in distinction means being able to assess your own energy by discerning whether it's lights-on or lights-off, then making choices from this perspective rather than simply out of habit. Habits can create automated "ruts" or pathways in our brain; which explains why it's imperative to become aware of the habits you have.

Those ruts can drive any of us to follow a habituated automatic behavior or action, instead of allowing us the freedom to make better choices in each moment. Choice equal distinction.

Think about the times you've automatically reached for an unhealthy snack, continued a behavior you didn't really like, or stopped yourself from doing something you knew would be healthy simply because it seemed *"too hard"* or just wasn't your automatic *"go-to"*.

Making distinctions involves noticing changes, even subtle ones, in your personal energy field. You can practice it by pausing to reflect and asking yourself,

> *Where is my energy right now? Energetically what's different today?*

Noticing what's different or what has changed will direct you toward more energy and creativity. To make room in your life for more creativity, ask yourself:

> *Do I love where I am and what I'm doing?*

If the answer is no, recreate a new vision for what you want and be open to the possibility for change. Focusing on that question will rekindle the creative spark.

> ◎ **Living in distinction is a signal to do more of what you love and less of what you don't love.**

Learn to delegate the tasks you don't love. Being aware of others' energy as well as your own will help you discover someone who loves doing the work you don't enjoy. (Rest assured, as much as you don't light up about something, there is someone else who does!). Delegation frees your energy so you can more readily make lights-on/lights-off distinctions as you go through the day.

Clarity in Action: Sharon's Story

Sharon, a successful graphic designer and entrepreneur who runs her own business, realized that even though she was doing work she loved, she was becoming drained. She was focusing more on holding on to her energy than she was on being creative.

Sharon noted the differences in her energy levels when she shifted her focus from patterns and routines draining her toward tasks lighting her up. Through this method she was able to discern quickly what parts of her work she wanted to continue doing and the parts where she needed help.

She began her analysis by looking at the overall flow pattern of a normal day. Sharon would start by meeting with a client to determine the requirements for their project then return to her studio to create five or six preliminary designs. She would then revisit the client with the sample designs to see what appealed and discuss any changes. After that, she would go back to the studio a second time to make the revisions, create a final design, and draw up an estimate.

Sharon asked herself, *do I love where I am and what I'm doing?* She saw there were two main aspects of her work bringing her joy: the freedom of being her own boss, and creating beautiful graphic pieces for her clients. All the scheduling and the back-and-forth travel to client meetings were tiring her and taking hours away from her design work. Being by herself in the quiet of her studio, immersed in the creative process, was what truly lit her up.

However, the other business processes were critical and still had to be done—just not by Sharon herself. As she became clear about which tasks drained her, she was able to write a job description incliuding everything on her lights-off list.

Still, she hesitated to hire someone for the job, assuming that if she didn't like a certain task, neither would anyone else. But despite these misgivings, she persevered and found Maggie. Maggie loved the idea of meeting with clients to present the preliminary designs, then coaching them through the choice process and feeding the information back to Sharon.

From the beginning, Sharon and Maggie worked so well together that they decided to form a business partnership. Since then they've expanded, becoming one of the top design firms in their city—a success neither could have achieved on her own. Using the *Get Clarity* process, Sharon went from working alone and lights-off to working lights-on with a partner.

Two years into their partnership, Sharon and Maggie realized that neither of them were lights-on about accounting, so they hired someone for that position. Now, the design process, client meetings, and financial functions are all being handled by people who love what they do.

Navigation Tools: Your Ideal Day

Sharon used the Ideal Day exercise to help her figure out which activities were lights-on for her and which were energy drains. With the list of lights-on clues you identified in the "Refine Your Focus" exercise to guide you, write a description of your Ideal Day.

My Ideal Day:

- Where am I living and working?

- What time do I get up and go to bed?

- What do I feel like?

- Who is with me, or helping me?

- Who is on my team, both at home and at work?

Scan your personal and near fields using the Energy Meter. Note everything that registers 7 or above and include these elements in your vision of your Ideal Day. Add anything else that gives you lights-on energy.

Now go back and look for any people, places, activities, or situations that are draining your energy. Make a lights-off task list to help you delegate the things that drain you.

Chapter Six

Practicing Sacred Selfishness

Sacred (sa kr d) adj. worthy of respect; venerable.
—The American Heritage Dictionary

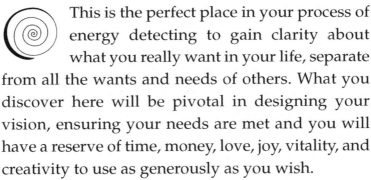 This is the perfect place in your process of energy detecting to gain clarity about what you really want in your life, separate from all the wants and needs of others. What you discover here will be pivotal in designing your vision, ensuring your needs are met and you will have a reserve of time, money, love, joy, vitality, and creativity to use as generously as you wish.

We call this notion *sacred selfishness*. To function fully and effectively, you must serve yourself, and your vision, before serving others. It is like those in-flight emergency instructions that tell you to put on your own oxygen mask before you try to help other passengers with theirs, so you both stay alive. You cannot give to others if your personal energy field is drained and you are an empty vessel. Being a martyr serves no one.

Even if martyrdom seems celebrated in our culture: *"Oh, I'm so busy! I barely sleep. I work so much; I'm constantly hustling. I can never seem to find enough time to get to my stuff; every thing else comes first."* It's almost as if *"I'm so busy (I work 20 yours a day)"* has become some sort of proud battle cry. Busy has become a badge of honor.

Cultivating sacred selfishness is an important part of learning how to hold your own energy field and preserve your vitality. If it seems odd for us to talk about being selfish in a book about partnership, hold any judgment for a moment. Imagine trying daily to hold yourself accountable for how you feel moment by moment and noticing what lights you up and what drains you; now imagine it was also your job to do the same thing for someone else. Feels heavy, doesn't it? Well it's not your job—your own energy is your job.

At *Clarity* we often say, *"Lights are an inside job."* When you're able to hold your energy field, it releases your responsibility for your partner's energy field (or happiness). That way you can both give to each other and be there for each other from a lights-on place.

When you hold your own energy field in a lights-on manner, by yourself and with another, you feel full and content, and able to be generous. It seems paradoxical to link selfishness and generosity, yet in the context of using your energy mindfully, it makes perfect sense.

> If you feel yourself going lights-off—losing energy—immediately stop and ask yourself "the Santa Claus question": **If I could have anything I wanted, what would that be?** Remember to answer as if anything is possible: be very specific even as you open your mind to all possibilities. Expansive thinking creates an energy field that is free of limitation.

Clarity in Action: Riley's Story

When Riley entered the Get Clarity retreat, she owned a very successful real estate marketing business. Her firm managed the entire sales process for developers as they created and built new housing projects. She gave the developers design ideas specifically appealing to buyers, created all the sales and marketing materials, and hired and managed the entire sales team.

Riley really loved this initial phase of launching a new project. However, she began to notice even with a lot of staff to help her, she was running herself ragged. In addition to work she loved, she had a philanthropic passion: she was in charge of an international non-profit relief project to help refugees. Riley was going in so many different directions she felt scattered and ungrounded and couldn't decide what was really important to her. Basically, everything she was doing lit her up, but it also exhausted her. Many of our entrepreneur clients can relate to this, having too many projects or opportunities exciting them at one time leaving them unable to focus—it's often referred to as *"Shiny Thing Syndrome."*

In a coaching session, Riley reviewed her daily schedule and assigned each task a rating on the Energy Meter. All of her daily tasks lit her up at 7 or above, so she had to make an even finer distinction and rate her tasks by "big lights"—9 or above. This process helped her distinguish what was most important to her, enabling her to focus her energy and attention.

When Riley was asked the Santa Claus question, she began sorting through all her daily activities. It was important for her to notice whenever she felt drained by one of her projects the project itself *was also experiencing an energy drain.* Her energy level had a ripple effect on everything around her. When she filled herself with energy, a field of possibility and generosity opened up.

Using the principle of sacred selfishness, Riley distilled her commitments down to the two she loved most: *being the visionary for her real estate business* and *the visionary for the overseas relief project.*

It also became clear what was draining her: continually running around raising funds and performing endless administrative errands without help. Her solution was to partner with a person who loved details. She hired an operations person for each of her projects so she could delegate those tasks.

Shifting from being a "control freak" to a "control tower" enabled Riley to perform her lights-on role as the visionary. And now, because of her clarity and delegation, both projects have doubled in effectiveness and capacity. Being very clear about what she wanted—her vision—before figuring out how to accomplish it conserved Riley's energy for getting the job done.

Navigational Tools:
The Santa Claus Question

The Santa Claus Question is one of our most effective tools for figuring out what you want. But often people find it hard to answer honestly: they don't feel deserving enough to dream big. Or they don't want to choose and they want it all. To assist you in thinking expansively, enlist the help of your partner. Or, together select a friend to help both of you. Pick someone who promises not to comment on or give opinions about your answers. This person's job will be to ask you, *"If I were Santa Claus and could give you anything you wanted, what would that be?"* repeating the question until you run out of answers.

- Take time to explore each of your responses to the questions so that you get a true reading of your energy.

- Ignore the *"how-to."* This is key. If you go to the how-to—the strategy and tactics for achieving your vision—before you have clearly defined the *"what"*—you will deplete your energy and block the flow of the visioning process by getting stuck in the details.

- Ask your friend to be a scribe and write down only your lights-on answers. If you catch yourself talking about what you don't want, go back and *state only what you do want.* This is important, often we can easily tell others what we don't want *"I don't want to struggle. I don't want to be unhappy, I don't want to…"* but creating a list of our wants is harder. Once you get the hang of it, you and your partner will start to notice shifts by focusing on what you do want. Make sure your scribe writes down all your lights-on responses even if they seem random and disconnected from each other. You may discover some seemingly random thought opens the door to a new energetic perspective on whatever you are envisioning. Repeat the same process for your partner to discover his or her lights-on clues. This is a playful and creative partnership exercise.

Chapter Seven

Designing Your Vision and Creating a Shared Vision

When master sculptors make figures out of wood or stone,

they do not introduce the figure into the wood,
but chisel away the fragments that concealed the figure;
they give nothing to the wood, rather they take
away from it, letting fall beneath the chisel the outer layers,
removing the rough covering, and then what
had lain hidden beneath shines out

—Meister Eckhart, Theologian and Christian Mystic

Designing your vision is the next step in preparing to move into the energetic flow of your journey. You are building on the clues you've been gathering by noticing what you want to take with you—whatever is lights-on—and the lights-off elements you want to leave behind.

Basically, you are beginning to load your cargo onto your metaphorical sailboat and build the navigation system guiding it. Your cargo is composed of the people, situations, activities, objects, and thoughts energetically serving your vision. The navigation system we've used successfully for many years simply consists of your lights-on and lights-off responses to your cargo. It will steer you through the necessary course corrections as you move into the flow of the river.

This skill of being able to tune into the energetic signals and vitality clues showing up in you (and your environment) is what we call *high noticing*. Your *"near field"*, which includes the people around you and your physical surroundings, mirrors the energetic signals you are sending and receiving. This is the dance of partnership. Your outer world reflects your inner state, in other words.

If you feel confusion coming from the near field, there may be some form of confusion and internal clutter in your thoughts. You attract what you think about. Conversely, if you feel clear, a feeling of clarity will be reflected back to you by your surroundings.

Clarity in Action: Virginia's Story

Virginia worked in a division of a large international company. Eight years of sitting at a desk and working on a computer had resulted in physical stress: stiffness, joint pain, and neck aches. She enjoyed her work but realized that her body was signaling she was ready for a change.

She became interested in the exercise system known as Pilates. She hired a personal Pilates trainer and started exercising two days a week. Almost instantly she noticed big differences: the pain and stiffness in her body eased, and she was more comfortable. And while she was exercising, she experienced a very pleasant sense of timelessness. She would look at her watch and be surprised to see hours had gone by. Paying close attention to all the energetic shifts within herself, Virginia soon became clear she wanted to practice Pilates full time, as an instructor. What had started as a simple health regime had provided a lights-on clue to a new career.

Virginia began volunteering at a friend's Pilates studio several evenings a week. She discovered while she was in the studio, she was lights-on, and wondered what it would be like to stop working in the corporate world, become certified as a Pilates instructor, and open her own exercise studio. Would she enjoy being an entrepreneur, or would turning her hobby into a business "knock her lights out"?

She continued to pay high attention to her energy both in her day job and in the studio. As she became clear about her passion for her new work, her confusion dissipated, and she could see her next step was to sign up for Pilates instructor training.

Realizing it would take about a year to make the transition, Virginia began designing her vision by creating a plan. She would keep her day job so she would have financial security, then focus the rest of her time, money, and energy on her new vision. Her plan allowed time to complete the teacher training required to become certified, and to design her studio, purchase needed equipment, and line up clients.

Two years after she created her vision and put her plan into action, Virginia quit her job and opened a studio that was already fully booked with clients. Today, she and her business are thriving, as she continues to live her vision, having also added a marriage partner to share in her joy.

Clearing Clutter

Designing a vision is as much about removing obstacles to realizing your dream as it is about having the dream in the first place.

Your outer surroundings reflect your inner state, and sometimes you can't see your vision clearly until you've cleared away clutter—anything in your personal field or near field that drains your energy and stops you from moving forward. Sometimes what prevents you from going into flow is, quite literally, physical clutter.

For some people, one of the most important steps in designing a vision is rolling up their sleeves and cleaning house. Up until now the focus of this book has been on creating a healthy internal mental environment but this next step changes your physical field. Literally, it's time to clean your physical environment. If this sounds familiar, your task is to identify and remove all the accumulated stuff in your home and/or office that doesn't light you up. If you're in a partnership it's a good idea to discuss the items affecting both of you. Your partner may not like getting rid of their sofa from college, simply because it doesn't light you up! This can be a very powerful step: for our client, Arlene, clearing clutter and simplifying her life made all the difference in creating flow.

Clarity in Action: Arlene's Story

Arlene wanted a new vision and new changes in her life when she began the Clarity process. She lived in a large home filled with many beautiful objects—collections with meaning and value to her. She had a home office was filled with files and paperwork from her business. Arlene also had a second office, outside her home, where she met clients, which was stuffed with paper, files, and business equipment. On top of that, she also had a weekend beach house.

The realization that her collections felt like too much "stuff" was a big clue to what was draining Arlene's energy and blocking her ability to move forward with ease and clarity. With her possessions spread over three different locations, she spent a lot of time searching for things. This unproductive and aimless use of her time drained her, and she felt scattered and unable to decide what she wanted to do next. It became clear to Arlene clutter was creating confusion and lack of flow.

Her first step was to begin clearing the clutter. She spent time in each location noting everything calibrated at less than 7.5 on the Energy Meter. As she walked through her outside office, Arlene noticed the space itself did not light her up; on the contrary, it drained her energy. She decided to downsize into one office space. That task seemed so overwhelming, however, so she hired a professional organizer to help her sort, systematize, and consolidate everything into her home office. Once she was able to find things more easily, Arlene began to feel clear, focused, and energized.

A year later, Arlene realized traveling between her main house and the beach house wasn't lighting her up anymore. She decided to sell the beach house and again brought in the professional organizer to help her downsize. She saved only the things she really loved from the beach house and brought them back to her main house.

Over time, Arlene realized she still felt overwhelmed by her possessions, so she embarked on yet another clearing process. She formed a temporary and strategic partnership with a feng shui practioner. It took about a year to sort through and consolidate her belongings and clear out items that drained her energy or inhibited the flow of energy in her home.

When it was done, Arlene noticed she felt very clear and fully present. She could walk into her home—and home office—and be focused, directed, and ready for business.

Now both her life and business have flow. Arlene lives and works with clarity and ease, surrounded only by things that light her up.

Navigational Tools: Designing Your Vision

Designing a vision is a step-by-step process incorporating all the tools you've learned so far. Practice high noticing and clearing clutter to eliminate anything not supporting or facilitating moving your vision forward, and then use the Ideal Day exercise to gather lights-on clues for making a Vision Map. Your partner, using this same process, creates his or her own Vision Map. Then together you can create a Shared Vision Map.

Practice High Noticing:

- Pay close attention to what shows up in your personal and near fields. See where there is clarity, and where there is confusion, or a feeling of being drained or exhausted.

- List the things energizing you and create clarity, as well as those causing a drain and creating confusion.

Clear Away Clutter:

- Scan your personal and near fields with the Energy Meter. Remove anything registering lights-off energy or create a strategy for dealing with it that will bring you to lights-on energy.

- Remember to check in with your partner on this one! If they share your living space, they'll likely have input.

Experience Your Ideal Day:

- Using the description of your Ideal Day from the Chapter Five Navigational Tools, do everything you listed in the exercise.

- Pay attention to where your thoughts are; what energetic flow you are feeling; and what is happening in your near field.

- Be aware of additional clues that may show up during the day.

- Write down your experiences in your journal, and add any new lights-on clues to your vision list.

Create a Shared Vision Map:

POWERFUL PARTNERSHIP FIELDS

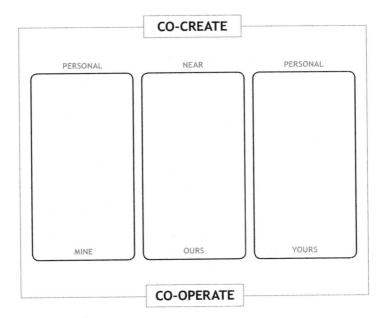

*"Out beyond the idea of wrongdoing and rightdoing
there is a field. I'll meet you there.*
~Rumi

- Using the above graphic, list all the lights-on clues from each partners interview in the separate Personal fields boxes. Then list all of the shared visions in the Near field box.

- Review all the lights-on clues you have discovered so far and create a Shared Vision Map— a visual image of what you both want to create in your lives. Don't worry if you are not an artist; many people cut images out of magazines and paste them onto paper or poster board. These can be things you want to create individually, or items you desire to create together; things like a family, a remodel in your home, adopting pets, types of vacations, or even how you both want the next few years to look.

- The form is not important: you are simply putting together images speaking to the essence of your vision. Expressing your dreams graphically or pictorially taps into the qualities of the right brain, allowing you to connect to your shared vision in a deeper way.

- Place your map in a prominent place so you can both see it often. Having a visual representation of your shared vision will keep you focused and energized as you cast off on your journey together.

Imagine the powerful energy of someone holding all the things you want to create in your life as importantly as what they want to create for themselves? That's truly powerful partnership!

PART III

Cast Off

Chapter Eight

Choosing Intention, Creating Attraction

Let yourself be silently drawn by the stronger pull of what you really love.
—Jalal-Uddin Rumi, Turkish Sufi Mystic Poet

 You are now casting off on the journey with a deep understanding of where you both want to go, individually and together. You have assembled your lights-on clues and created your Shared Vision Map. You are clear on your shared direction and what you each want to create. Guided by this vision, you must now both be intentional in everything you do. When you're intentional in your thoughts, words, and actions, you send out energy attracting to you the people, situations, and material support you need to reach your goal.

An intention is a strong purpose or vision driven by effective action and direction. Being intentional is a vital aspect of the *Get Clarity* process. It builds a co-creative field of energy with the divine in which all things are possible. Every aspect of your life is positively impacted when you approach it with conscious intention. A heart-connected vision, coupled with an intention, shifts your attention to the actions and behaviors leading you to a fully realized life.

It is easy to fall into the trap of living unconsciously. But having clarity requires you to be fully conscious—present and aware of all your thoughts and actions. Choosing intention is one of the most powerful methods for achieving your vision. Clear intentions equal clear results.

When you set your intentions every day, you will cease to be an accidental tourist on your life's journey.

Focus on the Shared Vision

As we've said, a successful partnership journey, whether personal or business, requires thoughtful planning and blending of each partner's individual vision.

Any partnership journey begins with three visions—each partner's individual vision and then the shared vision. It is important that all partners know and respect each other's individual vision. If either partner has to suppress or discard their individual vision, the energy gets draining and leads to compromising, which is a situation where no one gets what they want.

However, the primary focus and attention is on creating the shared vision—the vision that is truly the most powerful. Don't ignore the individual visions, but hold space for these outlier visions for another time.

Clarity in Action: Molly's and William's story

Molly and William have lived in Las Vegas for many years. William is a very successful leader in a Las Vegas show—a great, well paying gig for a musician. While recognizing that they would be living in Las Vegas for many years, they each dreamed of life elsewhere.

Molly an accomplished musician in her own right and also a yoga master dreamed of creating yoga videos. She felt strongly that to fully realize her dreams she needed to live in Los Angeles, the creative capital of the world.

William grew up on the East Coast and had a successful career in the vibrant music scene there. He longed to return to that idyllic creative time.

They both longed for a spiritual community of like-minded people to associate with. Even knowing Las Vegas was to be their home for many years, the conflicting dreams kept both of them from focusing on building on their dreams where they were.

When they began to focus on the things they wanted to create together—creative projects, starting a family, spiritual community and a secure financial future, they realized they could, together, create that vision in Las Vegas.

It's now many years later, William continues to grow in his position with the long-running musical show. Molly has several entrepreneurial ventures—yoga videos, organic tea company and joint projects with William. Plus, they have a daughter. Their spiritual community has grown in a way they never expected. Once they quit looking elsewhere, they discovered the advantages of living in Las Vegas.

When asked about those different bi-coastal visions, Molly says, *"I can barely remember feeling that way. We love it here and have everything we need."*

In Molly and William's story, all choices are contained. Molly is a yoga master. Willam is an accomplished musician. Together they also compose music to illustrate yoga movements for early childhood education. They love their co-creative energy.

Navigational Tools: Setting Your Intention

The energy and the focus of your thoughts are an important part of setting an intention. When you set your intention, it is important to think and speak in terms of what you want rather than what you don't want.

- Beware of negative thoughts and speech patterns, such as: *I should, I ought to, I have to.* These can undermine your intentions. *"In every meeting I'm in today, my intention is to be fully engaged"*, is a more empowering thought than: *"Since I have to be in meetings all day, I should try and pay attention."*

- Set clear intentions daily by using the template *My intention for today is* _____ .
  A positive example would be: *"My intention for today is to make healthy food choices at all meals"*. This phrasing gives you direction and fosters action.
  (A negative example would be *"My intention for today is to not eat junk food"*. This phrasing can create inertia by emphasizing what you don't intend to do without saying what you do intend to do.)

Create Attraction

As you begin to live every day intentionally, following your lights-on energy with your thoughts, actions and behaviors, you will notice people are responding to you with similar energy. Energy attracts like energy. So, in your thoughts, words, and actions, be very clear about what you want to attract into your life.

As we said in Chapter Three Looking for Lights On, when you focus your thoughts and actions in a calm, energized, lights-on state, you will look and feel different, and reflect, act, and attract differently. You will have an overall balanced, lighter, more up-lifted appearance—an inner glow. You will feel more energized and move through your daily life with more grace and ease. As a result, you will act differently. Your actions will be purposeful and aligned with your vision. You will attract more of what you want into your life.

> **The old paradigm was to wait until circumstances were perfect and then act. The new paradigm is to act as if what you want is already a reality, in order to create the circumstances. If you live it like you want it to be, you will attract to you what you need to take your vision to the next level. True attraction is effortless and joy-filled.**

When you send your *attractor energy* out into the world, you will notice coincidences and syn-chronicities appear. Out of the blue, the person who can provide information for the next step in your journey will turn up at a party or networking event you attend. You are thinking about someone, and the phone rings and it's that person on the line. Watch for synchronous events to occur. These are clues you are truly in energetic flow toward your vision. They guide you in the direction you need to go.

Clarity in Action: Justin's Story

Justin is a very successful businessman. Over several years he had developed a multi-unit service business with locations in several cities. A few years after he began growing his business, he went into a partnership with Stan, intending to share the workload.

Within a very short time, Justin and Stan began to disagree about almost everything. For a couple of years they tried to work out their differences, but nothing changed. Their behavior toward one another began to affect all their employees; creating a toxic work environment. Surprisingly, in spite of this toxic environment, the business continued to make money, so both partners were reluctant to make necessary changes.

By following the *Clarity* process, Justin became very clear about what he passionately wanted for himself, his family, and his employees. He returned to his work with renewed energy and an intention to create a new way of working. Every day he began to practice the *Clarity* tools and went into the office with renewed energy, a clear intention, and a belief that a winning scenario could be created for every-one, including his partner.

At one point, his wife sent us a thank you note because her husband was using words like *"every-day miracles"*, *"intention"* and *"gratitude"*, and he had a renewed sense of energy and commitment to make things happen differently.

Even though Justin and Stan still disagreed about most things, Stan noticed the change in Justin's energy and commented on it. Their conversations became less combative, and several key employees told Justin how much better it felt in the office without all the negative energy.

Then synchronicity appeared.

One of Justin's lights-on clues was a desire to provide consulting to other businesses doing similar work. He believed he had a lot to offer and set an intention to let people know he would be available sometime in the future. Suddenly, two different people approached him about consulting work. He had not advertised his services nor told anyone about his vision.

Just being lights-on about the thought of con-sulting opened the door for synchronicity to enter.

As time went on, Stan began his own *Clarity* journey, and he and Justin found a way to dissolve their partnership in a manner energizing to them both.

Navigational Tools:
Become an Attractor

Using the Energy Meter, assess the quality of your interactions, your relationships, and what you are attracting to your vision. Distinguish between attracting drama (0 on the meter), which is energy-draining, and increasing energy (10 on the meter), which is vitalizing.

- Be aware when your life seems to move forward effortlessly, as if you were being pulled along by an unseen current. Think of that current as the attraction factor.

- Notice how quickly your lights-on clues manifest into reality. Observe when people show up just as you need them, and information appears to guide your next step.

- Recognize and note intentions you have set in motion attracting people and information to you.

- Write down all examples of synchronous events occurring in your life. Keep a synchronicity journal.

Chapter Nine

Observing Resistance, Shifting Attention

The real voyage of discovery consists not in seeking new landscapes, but in having new eyes.
—Marcel Proust, Author

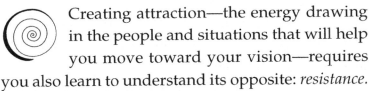 Creating attraction—the energy drawing in the people and situations that will help you move toward your vision—requires you also learn to understand its opposite: *resistance.*

Resistance is the magnetic energy field you want to steer away from. Learning to pay attention to resistance as it appears on your journey is critical for moving your thoughts and actions toward attraction. As you get a feel for the dynamic between attraction and resistance, you will be equipped to watch for the clues to help you shift your attention to doing what is necessary to get back into forward flow.

Energetic resistance can come from external forces blocking your progress, such as a person or situation, or it can come from within—from your own conscious unconscious actions. You will experience resistance as a slowing of your progress—a lack of energetic flow. Sometimes there will be so much resistance it will stop your forward momentum completely.

It's important to pay attention to resistance when it occurs, and to use the information it contains to reassess your course of action. If you find yourself saying, *"I'm going to do this no matter what,"* or *"I'm going to do this even if it kills me,"* you will know that your attention and focus have gone into resistance instead of following your lights-on energy toward your vision.

This energetic resistance will continue until you figure out what it is telling you.

Is it taking your focus off committing yourself to actions that are aligned with your dream? Is it sending you a stop-and-reevaluate signal?

Hard work and diligence are essential in reaching a goal, but excessive stress and pressure lead only to exhaustion, and divert you from your path.

Many times in life we are called to do difficult things to further our dreams and goals. It's not that every sign of difficulty or effort is a clue that you are on the wrong path.

We are merely suggesting that importance of learning to pay close attention so you can be aware of clues as they appear. Discerning which clues spell resistance will help you make conscious choices about what action is required to best accomplish your vision. Ineffective action, or wasted effort, can be not only be draining but a deterrent as you travel down the path toward your dreams.

Clarity in Action: Eric and Britt's Story

Eric and Britt—two successful entrepreneurs married in their late 30s having both developed successful businesses.

Eric's business was very financially successful and his focus was only on the bottom line; the profits. Britt's business, while successful, was not as profitable because her focus was more on the philanthropic aspects. Eric's vision was for Britt to be the homemaker since it was his business that supported their quality lifestyle.

When they both felt the resistance from their different goals and expectations, they reached out for coaching. During the coaching Eric recognized the resistance he was causing in the flow of their relationship and began to shift his attention to how he could support Britt's dream. This became part of their shared vision to give back. And to do it through their partnership of equals.

Clarity in Action: Ann and John's Story

Ann and John were relocating to a new urban area and had created a vision map to guide their search for a live/work space.

After months of touring properties close to their vision but not quite a match, they came across one that really captured their imagination. It was a carriage house behind a Victorian house to which it had once belonged. Though currently used to garage a classic car collection, it was listed as a potential residence.

Ann and John fell in love with the huge open space, the high ceilings and brick walls, and the location near downtown. The building sat on a large lot that offered unique privacy in the heart of the city. They were so excited by the potential to create a truly unique space that they hired an architect to do a preliminary design while they proceeded with the legalities of closing the deal.

The first clue of resistance came when the seller tried to insert a *"Buy As Is"* clause in the contract and pushed for a quick transfer of possession. Ann and John were not concerned, however, and negotiated a contract that gave them time to do the necessary inspections.

The second challenge they encountered was discovering that the water and sewer lines for the carriage house had never been separated from those of the main house. They would need to get permits from the city and hire a contractor to bring water from the city lines under the street. Still, Ann and John were not deterred; they knew there would be work involved in renovating an old building. They just knew that when it was completed they would have a wonderful little oasis in the city.

During this time, they were also selling their home in another state. When they made the offer on the carriage house, they thought their old home had sold. But just before closing, the buyer backed out, and Ann and John were forced to negotiate a later closing date on the property they were buying. This was one clue they knew they needed to pay attention to. But soon they had another buyer and were back on track.

And then they visited City Hall and found the carriage house was not zoned for residential use. It would require a hearing before the zoning board to secure permission. While it was likely their request would be approved, it would be several weeks before the hearing could be scheduled. At this point, the lack of flow was so obvious to Ann and John they stopped the sale, forfeiting the investment with the architect, and began their search anew.

But as it happened, during the months Ann and John had spent trying to buy the carriage house, another property had come on the market that fit their vision perfectly.

Even better, it was available for immediate occupancy. This time, the sale went through without a hitch, and they were able to move in quickly.

Navigational Tools: Noticing Resistance

The overarching message from Ann and John's experiences is that when moving forward toward your vision; it's essential to be aware of the clues you are receiving. These clues are vital feedback so, if necessary, you can adjust your strategy. Ask yourself:

- Are we being shown signs of flow and ease?

- Are we struggling with challenges that drain our energy?

- Is what's showing up taking our focus off actions aligned with our dream?

- Is it draining our energy?

- Is it sending us a stop-and-evaluate signal?

- Are there people or situations blocking our progress.

- Are we finding ourselves doing something out of obligation or fear rather than out of enthusiasm and trust?

You might want to make a note of any clues showing up—and write down your answers to these questions—so you won't overlook something potentially slowing or halting your progress.

Shift Your Attention

The way out of resistance, whether from an external source or your own internal dialogue, is to consciously shift your attention. You can move closer to making your vision a reality by shifting your focus to the thoughts and the actions that bring forward flow.

On the Clarity journey, the concept of *"change your thinking, change your life"* is all about the lights-on energy you bring to a situation. It's about the choices you make in your own thinking. If you focus your thoughts and attention on resistance and the struggle you feel against it, you will only bring more lights-off energy into your field.

You cannot make viable decisions about which actions to take from a low-energy mindset. You are far more likely to make decisions aligned with your vision and take appropriate action if you view your choices through the filter of lights-on energy.

The power of changing your thoughts to create a different reality has now been established scientifically. Studies in cellular biology and neuroscience show the cells in your body and the neural pathways in your brain are highly impacted by your thoughts, *both positive and negative.* Each cell membrane receives a signal from the environment, and the behavior of the cell is affected by your brain's interpretation of signals.

> **Neuroplasticity:** Where you place your attention creates new neural pathways. The power of the brain to change in response to the external and internal environment is known as **neuroplasticity**. Directing attention away from negative thoughts toward positive ones can create permanent positive changes; *not only in your thinking but in your physiology as well.* When you continually focus on positive thoughts and qualities like kindness, compassion, and generosity the brain actually rewires itself so that it skews toward a more optimistic outlook, and the old, well-worn ruts or paths of negative thinking become more difficult to access.

Changing any negative habit, including negative thinking, takes sustained, conscious effort. But neuro-scientists report re-patterning the brain can take place in as little as three weeks, creating an atmosphere for growth, creativity, and lights-on behavior. When you continually shift your attention to the people and things lighting you up, new neural pathways are formed increasing your ability to stay lights-on.

Clarity in Action: Joann's Story

Following a long held vision, Joann opened a yoga studio that she operated successfully for several years. Like many creative entrepreneurs, she began to realize that managing the studio was draining her energy. She loved teaching classes and training other yoga instructors, but she did not like running the business.

Joann considered different strategies: hiring a manager, selling the studio, finding a managing partner/investor. She also considered closing the studio altogether, but she could not bring herself to abandon her loyal clients, or give up on her original dream.

She developed a new vision of using her yoga reputation to produce a local weekly television show that would present the life-enhancing practice of yoga to a wider audience. She envisioned the freedom of presenting her expertise in a way that did not keep her tied to a physical location.

Her one stumbling block was that she remained focused for months on how managing the studio was preventing her from following her bigger dream, and she couldn't let go of the idea she had to keep the studio open even if she no longer wanted to run it. Joann's old thought patterns continued to drain her energy and block her ability to see other possibilities.

When she finally realized her resistance was preventing her from realizing her dream, Joann committed to shifting her focus to her more expansive vision. Every time she began to think about what she couldn't do, she immediately refocused her thoughts on her intention to create something new.

Although she was still involved with daily management tasks, Joann felt more energized because she began to see possibilities. Holding the vision of what she wanted to create, she was able to see her current situation in a more forgiving light. New ideas began to percolate, and it occurred to her that she could create a new way of serving her long-term clients. Rather than sell the studio and the brand name she had spent so long developing, she realized she could trade on her brand to launch her expanded venture.

Joann didn't need her own studio to continue serving her clients; she could rent other studios in which to hold classes. She also saw that closing the studio didn't mean failure. She was simply expanding and evolving her business. Shifting her attention to this expanded vision every time she got stuck in feelings of limitation enabled her to see new ways of achieving her dream.

Navigational Tools:
Shifting Your Attention

As Joann's experience illustrates, consciously shifting your attention to lights-on thoughts and behaviors creates energetic flow. This is a good time to use rapid discovery and rapid recovery.

- Ask yourself, *"Where are my thoughts right now?"* If they are coming from fear, doubt, or some other negative energy, immediately turn your attention to something positive. To find something positive to focus on, think of someone or something for which you are grateful. Feeling and expressing gratitude brings lights-on energy into your system. Looking at your vision map and experiencing the energy of what you have envisioned helps you shift your thoughts.

- Keep notes or write in your journal about what happens to your energy when you shift your attention to something positive. Over time, you will begin to notice that you are less likely to get caught up in old, lights-off thoughts and you are able to shift to more effective thoughts much more rapidly.

Chapter Ten
Navigating Choice Points

Once you replace negative thoughts with positive ones,
you'll start having positive results.
—Willie Nelson, Singer Philosopher

Every outcome in present time is the result of a decision made at a choice point, or pivotal moment, in the past. Our choices create our current reality. From moment to moment, situations arise that require us to make choices. The way in which we focus our attention in those instances is what we call *"navigating choice points."* By navigating through choice points, or transitions (which at times may seem perplexing or stressful), these are actually key opportunities to consider different possibilities and make decisions that move you closer to your vision.

In daily life, as on the *Get Clarity* journey, divergent channels are constantly appearing, requiring choices on everything from what to eat and what to wear to where to live and how to communicate an idea. All these choice points require focused attention. In every instance, the goal is to choose above-the-line thoughts and actions—those that are energizing and solution-oriented—rather than under-the-line thoughts and actions that are draining and problem-focused.

On this journey, you are clearly seeking trans-formation and change. So what does it mean in the action phase of the journey, when it's time to launch your vision? The word *"transform"* will give you a clue. Trans is Latin for *"change"*; to transform is to change your form, or state. And in order to trans-form, you have to "come undone" and reform in a new way.

Most of our formal education and training fails to address the issue of change, and few of us learn enough about deep change to be comfortable with it. And today, transition, transformation, and change are occurring more rapidly than at any other time in history. This acceleration makes it imperative to learn new skills for rapidly redesigning your guiding vision and the strategy to achieve it as you are faced with choice points.

Just in the past decade, the deluge of information offered by new technology requires us to become more fluid and adaptive in our decision-making than our predecessors. A century ago, when there were fewer choice points, with more time in between them, humans adapted to change in concert with natural cycles—the rhythm of waking and sleeping, the flow of seasons, birth and death. Today, however, we no longer have the leisure to wait for change to occur naturally.

In order to navigate the rest of the Get Clarity journey with ease and grace—to find it exciting, not frightening—there is something you need to know: transition is a natural part of the change process.

Change creates a liminal zone, an *"in between"* or threshold, in which you're no longer where you were but not yet where you're going. Visions by their very nature are constantly evolving. They morph or shape-shift as information is added or subtracted.

A key skill for successful journeying is learning to navigate this transition zone—to be comfortable with uncertainty and living the mystery, as you follow your vision. This requires trusting once you have a clear strategy for navigating choice points, a new, more evolved vision will emerge to guide you on the next leg of your journey.

On the *Get Clarity* Attention Guide at the end of this chapter, the transition line is the bridge between above-the-line and under-the-line behaviors and thoughts. Every time you shift your attention from under-the-line to above-the-line, you cross through this zone and can experience some or all of the behaviors common to transition: discomfort, frustration, shift, transformation, challenge, and paradox. When you find yourself sensing any of these experiences, it is a clue you are at a choice point, and you can choose to take your attention above or below the line.

> A key skill for successful journeying is learning to navigate the transition zone—being relaxed with being in between and comfortable with living the mystery as you follow your vision.

The transition zone is the zone of transformation, where the choices you make determine the results of your actions.

Above-the-line choices are energizing, passionate, and solution focused, while under-the-line choices simply continue old draining patterns which tend to be problem-focused resulting in limited possibilities and stagnation. To stay true to your vision, it is essential to focus your choices above the line and choose passion and lights-on.

Clarity in Action: Stan's Story

We mentioned Stan earlier in Justin's story. Prior to becoming Justin's partner, Stan had his own successful business for several years. Although he was successful, he hated the management and marketing involved in building and maintaining the revenue and client base. What he did love and was very good at doing was delivering the technical services to his

customers. When he and Justin were discussing becoming partners, Stan was excited by the possibility
of turning the management and marketing over
to Justin and devoting all his time to being the
technician and taking care of the customers.

Shortly after they began operating under the
new partnership agreement, they disagreed about
almost everything to do with how to manage the
business, how to market their services, how to train
and develop employees, basically how to do everything except customer service. Stan and Justin would
spend hours creating an understanding about some
new aspect of the business. Justin would leave the
meeting believing they were in agreement. Stan
would leave the meeting and not follow through on
what was agreed upon. And then they were back
into arguing or not communicating at all. This went
on for several years.

As Stan began to understand and apply the *Get
Clarity* principles, he realized he didn't want to do
the management of the business, but he also had a
huge need to control anything done. If he didn't
have control, he was fearful of the effect someone
else's management would have on his income. Even
though Stan was making more money than he had
in his previous business, he couldn't let go of the
fear and trust issues of having Justin be responsible
for managing. This need to control all aspects kept
him fearful of anything Justin suggested or attempted

to put into place. He would then become distrustful and doubting about all of it. Obviously, this would lead to more lack of trust, an inability to communicate and as mentioned previously, it created a toxic work environment for everyone.

When Stan recognized how his behavior and thoughts were contributing to the situation, he began to use rapid discovery, rapid recovery whenever he found himself feeling out of control or fearful of the way the business was being managed. This didn't mean he didn't question or challenge anything he had questions about.

What did begin to happen, however, was after he received the information he requested, he focused his thoughts and energy on empowering Justin's decisions and trusting the process. This dramatically changed everything. By merely changing his energetic response to all of the management issues, the energy and flow of the business began to change.

Clarity in Action: Elaina's Story

As she began her *Get Clarity* journey, Elaina became aware her day-to-day decision-making was based on some long-standing shadow or under-the-line behaviors. With new awareness, she began to practice rapid discovery and rapid recovery every time she found herself reacting to events out of those old patterns.

Elaina had been divorced for several years and shared custody of her two children with her ex-husband. Many aspects of that arrangement had upset her for years, causing a lot of drama always leaving her frustrated and exhausted. After her *Clarity* training, she was determined to change her behavior. Before every interaction with her children's father, she started setting an intention to stay lights-on and to observe when her thoughts and behavior created drama and drained her energy, and to shift those thoughts immediately.

She also began to practice sacred selfishness, asking herself what she really wanted the custody arrangement to look like. When she examined her own behavior and outcomes, Elaine realized she sacrificed her own needs and desires when the initial custody agreement was drawn up. It turned out not only had the current agreement never worked for her, but it hadn't served the needs of her children either.

Focusing her attention on what she wanted helped Elaina renegotiate the existing custody arrangement to fit her needs and those of her children. She approached the situation from the new viewpoint *"all things are possible and there is a solution that would serve them all"*.

As often happens, when she focused her thoughts on keeping her energy and behavior above-the-line, the result was positive for everyone involved.

Navigational Tools: Navigating Choice Points

In every moment you are presented with choice points (either above or below the line). They are a universal constant. You are in charge of your choices. The challenge is to remain mindful and aware of what your options are and to always choose passion over pattern.

The *Get Clarity* Attention Guide below will help you determine whether or not you are choosing lights-on and passion when making decisions, or lights-off and limiting patterns.

If the words above the line match your actions, then you have chosen well. You can reference the bridge in the lower left corner of the *Get Clarity* Journey Map to see clearly how choosing above-the-line will keep you in flow.

Study the Attention Guide to find out where you are, and if it looks like you are stuck under-the-line, then shift your attention to an above-the-line thought or action, and get back into flow.

How to Use the Get Clarity Attention Guide

This guide and balance sheet is another *Get Clarity* tool to help you stay conscious and mindful about the choices you make and the behaviors you exhibit. When you are consciously aware, you will not intentionally make ineffective choices about your behaviors. This guide is put in chart form to make shifting your attention quick and easy.

Looking at the three Personal Field columns, there are forty-two words with corresponding symbols to the left, and there is a gray line dividing the words. The dividing line containing the words discomfort, confusion and anger is the transition line.

CLARITY ATTENTION GUIDE AND BALANCE SHEET

	INDIVIDUALS *What is my energy characterized by?*		PARTNERS *What is the energy I contribute to the partnership?*
◆	Effortlessness	Self Esteem	Co-creation
✳	High Noticing	Curiosity	Faith
●	Authenticity	Gratitude	Synergy
★	Dedication	Ruthlessness	Appreciation
◉	Enthusiasm	Celebration	Belonging
⌘	Excitement	Playfulness	Respect
■	Trust	Courage	Support
	Discomfort	Confusion	Anger
■	Fear	Denial	Greed
⌘	Exhaustion	Romance	Inequality
◉	Anxiety	Resentment	Isolation
★	Defiance	Self Pity	Blame
●	Self-Importance	Exactingness	Egotism
✳	Habituation	Doubt	Jealousy
◆	Overdoing	Martyrdom	Compromise

Lights On: The upper half of the guide contains a collection of twenty-one words representing above-the-line thoughts and behaviors. Energetically, above-the-line represents the field of possibilities. It is lights-on and effective. We also refer to above-the-line as the "light side". Actions initiated from this field are referred to as solution-focused and - effective as opposed to labels or judgment of good or right.

Lights Off: The lower half of the guide contains a collection of twenty-one words representing under-the-line thoughts and behaviors. Energetically, below the line represents the field of limits. It is lights-off and ineffective. We also refer to under-the-line as the shadow side or shadow behavior. Actions initiated from this field are referred to as problem-focused and ineffective as opposed to labels of bad or wrong.

Choice Points: The transition line is the bridge between the groups. Every time you shift your attention from under-the-line to above-the-line, you cross through this zone and can experience some or all of the behaviors common to transition: discomfort, confusion, anger, frustration, shift, transformation, challenge, and paradox. When you find yourself sensing any of these experiences, it is a clue that you are at a choice point and you can choose to take your attention above or below the line.

The symbols (i.e. ✳) are used to show a connection between a specific under-the-line behavior and a specific above-the-line behavior.

Example of how the vertical fields operate:

Fear (■ below) is the shadow side of **trust** (■ above) and discomfort (on the bridge) is the transitional experience.

Anxiety (◎ below) is the shadow side of **enthusiasm** (◎ above) and discomfort (on the bridge) is the transitional experience.

Defiance (★ below) is the shadow side of **dedication** (★ above) and discomfort (on the bridge) is the transitional experience.

Chapter Eleven
Launching Your Vision

Vision without action is a daydream.
Action without vision is a nightmare.
—Japanese Proverb

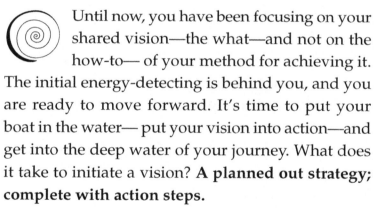

Until now, you have been focusing on your shared vision—the what—and not on the how-to— of your method for achieving it. The initial energy-detecting is behind you, and you are ready to move forward. It's time to put your boat in the water— put your vision into action—and get into the deep water of your journey. What does it take to initiate a vision? **A planned out strategy; complete with action steps.**

Action steps create the momentum to realize your vision; therefore, all of your action steps must be energizing and create excitement as you anticipate their result. This excitement makes the movement in the direction of your dream seem effortless—and timeless.

Almost without exception, our clients report as they launched their new vision, it seemed as if time stood still. This phase of the journey is a very energizing time, filled with a mixture of fear and excitement: you're taking a leap of faith. At this point, self-actualized people—those who are living the fulfillment of their dreams—say courage is the key component. They faced their fears and moved forward regardless. They don't say they became fearless, because it's not realistic to expect fearlessness. Faith comes with knowing any big step is bound to potentially create a feeling of fear; it's just using a mindset of shifting fear to trust. They moved forward with a vision and strategy, just as you are about to do.

Your tools for putting your vision into action are the vision map you made earlier—updated with your discoveries from previous exercises—and the action steps you are about to identify.

Once you have tuned up your vision and designed your strategy, you will be ready to launch. We use a model called a Bridge Plan to provide a structure for this stage. The Bridge Plan is dynamic and ever changing as you add and delete information over the course of your journey your Bridge Plans will shift to meet your goals. This dynamic model will help you maintain forward momentum as you swing between vision and action: *"Here is where I am now; here is where I want to be. What are the lights-on actions to get me there?"*

Clarity in Action—
Deborah and Scott's story

Deborah is an attorney, working full time in her practice while happily donating legal expertise to their community. Scott is a very successful consultant who travels frequently to meet with his clients. Nearing retirement age and both still loving their work, they tended to work more hours than they needed to financially.

They often talked about *"someday"* when they would slow down but had no vision in place for what that might look like. Scott was excited to retire and spend his time gardening and creating the landscape that he had always dreamed about. Deborah had no dream hobby, and she wanted to stay involved in her law practice. In coaching, they admitted that they had a fear of becoming bored and isolated, and out of sync with each other.

This created doubt, causing them to delay any flow toward their dream. The detour this doubt created showed up by relying totally on the advice of their financial plan rather than balancing the dream with the advice. They checked often to see what was the earliest date they could afford for Scott to retire fully while Deborah continued earning income. They wondered if was fair for one person to spend their savings and if it would create resentment...would greed enter the picture? So, in their mid-60's, they accessed coaching to create a shared vision for their future where both of their dreams were supported.

In coaching, they got clear about what each person wanted and then created a way to make it fun by making an image of a clock, artfully drawn with movable symbols of their interests. They clocked work time, Deborah at her office (a book) and Scott keeping the household running (a vacuum). Scott's gardening time (a palm tree) was matched to Deborah's community volunteer time (a hand). They allocated time for traveling (a car) and playing (a boat). They are fully living their vision and in their words, they are having *"the time of their life!*

Clarity in Action: Ellen's Story

When Ellen entered the *Get Clarity* retreat, she was exhausted and dragging through the day. She felt thoroughly depleted at the end of her usual seventy-hour workweek. Her career as director of a large non-profit organization was very demanding, and almost no energy left for her husband and two daughters.

While working downtown, she imagined a place where she could get a relaxing spa treatment during her lunch hour. But there was no spa near her office offering high-quality services in under an hour.

During her visioning session, Ellen became very clear that she wanted to start a downtown day spa within walking distance of most offices, where clients could receive unique, 25-minute "express" services.

Ellen's first action step was to share her vision with her husband whose support was necessary to initiate any change of this magnitude. A new business would be a risk to their financial security, and there was much to consider, since neither Ellen nor David had any experience as an entrepreneur. They had always been employees with job security and benefits.

Both were in their late forties and anticipated early retirement in ten years. But at the rate she was working, Ellen wasn't sure if she could physically and emotionally survive the stress of her job until retirement. It was imperative she find a way to make her dream come true without risking their life savings.

Ellen needed to do some in-depth research into what would be entailed in creating a spa. She spent the next year on this preparatory homework, gathering information about costs to start a day spa, the time it would take to become profitable, and the demographics for an ideal location. Ellen enjoyed

the research process and found it very energizing—
not at all like her regular job.

The next step was a coaching session in which
Ellen and David created a bridge plan, balancing
two key facts that had emerged from her research.
Creating a spa was going to be very costly, but at the
same time, Ellen's day-spa concept was at the fore-
front of an emerging business trend, making it, in
all likelihood, a savvy investment. Guided by both
the numbers and her passion to do it, Ellen went
ahead with initiating her vision.

Given her lack of entrepreneurial expertise, it
was a total leap of faith. She and David had fears
and challenges to face and overcome, but they were
confident their enterprise would be successful.
However, had Ellen tried to implement her strategy
before she was crystal clear about her vision, her
fear of the large investment and her lack of experience could have easily depleted her energy. Without
the pulling power of her vision, those fears could
have stopped before she even started. Imagine
sharing this brilliant idea with caring friends and
family who echo your own fears, worries, and
doubts and what it can do to your energy without
the powerful clarity behind vision and action steps!

As it was, Ellen's preparation paid off, and their
day spa opened to great success— clearly filling a
need in the downtown business community.

Navigational Tools:
Creating an Action Plan

Your next step toward launching your vision is to create an action plan:

- Hang your vision map where you can see it easily, as a constant reminder of where you are headed.

- Make a list of what you want to create in your life, combining all your lights-on clues from the previous chapters. Then, next to the list, write down the action steps needed to achieve each aspect of your vision.

- Create an action plan by prioritizing the action steps.

- Using the diagram below as a template, create a Bridge Plan. On the bridge, place the action steps that are energizing and will move you closer to your goal. If you have any action steps that are necessary but don't light you up, create a plan for delegating those actions to someone else.

**Here's where
you are now.**

**Here's where you
want to go—
Your lights-on vision.**

Fill in some action items on the bridge that are energizing and will move you closer to your vision.

Remember all action steps in present time should be in service to your vision. This avoids busy work.

PART IV

Correct Course

Chapter Twelve

Cruising through Challenges

By banishing doubt and trusting your intuitive feelings,
you clear a space for the power of intention to flow through.
—Wayne Dyer, Author and Speaker

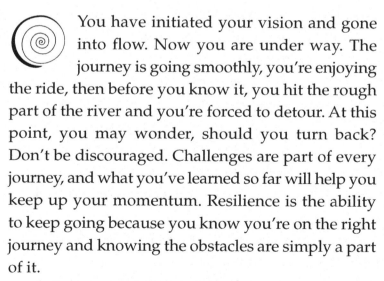 You have initiated your vision and gone into flow. Now you are under way. The journey is going smoothly, you're enjoying the ride, then before you know it, you hit the rough part of the river and you're forced to detour. At this point, you may wonder, should you turn back? Don't be discouraged. Challenges are part of every journey, and what you've learned so far will help you keep up your momentum. Resilience is the ability to keep going because you know you're on the right journey and knowing the obstacles are simply a part of it.

A detour can be any divergence from your intended route. On the *Get Clarity* Journey Map (located in the back of the book), it is symbolized by a logjam. Often you will hit a metaphorical logjam when you start sharing your dream with others. People are only too willing to offer advice and opinions on what you should be doing: *"That's a good idea but…"* or *"If I were you…" "Have you thought about…"* or *"You know what you need to do…"*

As you listen to this unsolicited advice, you may notice yourself starting to feel drained or irritable. There is a vast difference between wisdom and opinion.

No matter how well intended, others' opinions can knock your lights out and knock you off course.

Feedback, however, is a different story. It is a natural part of any energetic operating system. Feedback mirrors your enthusiasm back to you. It's an astute observer saying, *"I can see that your vision lights you up; tell me more about it."*

The way to get out of a logjam and back into flow is to find someone to give you effective feedback. Look for a person who is willing to suspend judgment and forgo opinions and advice, and simply report what they notice energizes you, then reflect it back to you.

A support person, who gives reflective feedback rather than projecting their unsolicited opinions and advice onto you, is an important *strategic ally*. It's very helpful to have at least one unbiased person like this on your team. Accurate feedback is not about someone else's ideas for you— only about what lights you up.

When you're faced with so-called *"friendly"* advice, remember not to take it personally. Well-meaning people may think they're "protecting" you, but they're really only projecting their own fears out of worry or concern for you. No matter how well meaning, both of those fall under the line and won't support your energy in moving forward. Don't let someone else's issues prevent you from initiating your vision.

Clarity In Action—
Gregory and Scott's story

Gregory and Scott were into the 4th year of a financially successful professional practice when it became obvious that neither of them were lights-on. Despite much attention being paid to pre-planning, once the partnership actually functioned, the incompatibilities became glaring and contentious.

Anger built to contempt and soon the partners could only communicate through 3rd parties. Thousands of dollars were spent with legal experts regarding how to divide the assets, and it became obvious the solution would have to come energetically rather than legally.

Both partners were interviewed separately to find their most positive solution with an agreement that blame would not be assigned, and focusing on strengths would be the guidance so both parties could be reasonably respected in the dissolution.

Gregory loved being the sole decision maker and team leader. Scott loved being able to come to work, treat his patients, and go home, leaving all business decisions behind. The surprising outcome, once both were brought together and asked to state what they admired about each other and to look at the individual ideal visions, was that a solution was immediately evident.

Gregory bought Scott's share of the practice becoming the solo decision maker, and Scott was hired as an employee freed from the business side of his profession. Both have remained friends and are grateful for the coaching that created a positive, professional dissolution.

Navigational Tools: Handling Detours

Detours are part of every *Clarity* journey. So what do you do when you hit one?

- *Return to your vision.* Refocus your energy by studying your vision map. Make sure you are looking at all the information through the filter of your vision so you are always giving it an energetic perspective. Keep your thoughts and actions above the line, as you create a strategy to get around the detour.

- If you need extra help with the process, find someone to act as a mirror to your vision. Ask them to give you accurate feedback, observing your lights-on energy as you state your vision. Take note of the feedback you're given and integrate into your new plan.

Doubt, Worry, and Negative Self-Talk

Sometimes it's not input from others knocking your lights out but your own monkey mind speaking to you with doubt or worry. Going through a major transition is seldom comfortable and may raise doubt and fear of the unknown.

> There can be moments on the **Clarity** journey when you are uncertain about what choice to make or what action to take. At such times it's essential not to lose sight of the fact that self-criticism, worry, and doubt will never give you accurate information on which to base decisions. They will only increase your fear and lead to inertia as you vacillate.

Doubt and worry take you out of the present moment and into overdramatizing past experiences—we call this *fictional history tripping*—or *inventing scary stories about the future.* We call that fictional future tripping. Monkey mind, that self-critical inner voice that conjures up worst-case scenarios, can stop you from pursuing your vision with running commentary like, *"What was I thinking?", "I can't possibly do this."* or *"This will never work."*

The way to deal with monkey mind is to **doubt your doubt, not your dream.** Fear takes over when you don't have enough information to make an intelligent choice. *Reduce your fear of the unknown by shifting your attention to gathering information.*

Clarity in Action:
Adam and Leigh's story

Adam and Leigh—theirs is a story of second marriages and blending households and the "house rules." Both having been married previously, entered into their marriage with a loving desire to learn from their experiences and create a new vision together.

Adam and Leigh have two children of their own, both pre-school age, and Adam has shared custody of his teenaged daughter who lives two weeks with him, and two weeks with her mother.

The vision for their home was to have it be a common ground; one embracing the comings & goings and varied interests of the wide age gap.

In the busyness of life, they neglected to clearly state the values that make them love their home.

Things such as standards of tidiness, healthy eating, electronic devices, homework & bedtimes, and who has the final say as to "house rules" when the household is shared by children from different marriages.

Leigh was given no authority over her step-daughter who was often messy and disrespectful when at their home every other week. Leigh was very clear with the rules for their two preschool children, but wasn't given any jurisdiction over the teenager. Adam just wanted to keep the peace until the week was over rather than support the vision of a common ground both Leigh and he had for their home. He almost hid out during the attempts by Leigh to engage in conversations and actions about it.

"Belonging" was also not a feeling any of them had, which isolated the stepdaughter and Leigh. The situation was creating doubt and worry.

In coaching they said it seemed like they were living in a nightmare rather than living in their dream life. They recognized to meet the challenges, big change was needed.

Part of the solution was to have a family team meeting using the *Get Clarity* check-in weekly as soon as the daughter arrived and include her, despite her objections. She belonged and was included as they planned their 2 weeks together with input from all. These meetings created a conscious intention. And despite the challenges and detours part of every partnership journey, Adam and Leigh's clear intention equaled clear results, and a more lights-on home for all.

Navigational Tools: Silencing Doubt and Self-Talk

When doubt, worry, or anxiety show up, you have options. You can make conscious, intentional choices once you know they exist. As a couple, it's important you have a safe space with each other to share your thoughts and get feedback to help you guide yourself back to being lights-on. Don't let negative self-talk take you out of the game. Take specific action:

- Quiet monkey mind by listening to what the doubt and fear are really saying. Write down the predominant thoughts. Read over your statements and decide if any of those concerns are real—and need to be addressed—or are only imagined.

- Face fear of the unknown by gathering as much information as you can. Armed with information you can pursue your vision with more certainty and less fear. If you are considering relocating, for example, you might explore the possibilities by searching the internet, consulting a realtor, studying a map, talking to people who live in the area, contacting the local Chamber of Commerce, investigating community services, and looking into employment opportunities.

Shadow Patterns

Shadow patterns are energy patterns, largely unconscious, which stop you from being in flow. Shadow behaviors are a metaphor for information hidden in the shadows from sight and cognitively difficult to see. We each have them but if you're not aware of them, they can prevent you from realizing your full potential.

Light patterns are defined as whatever energizes you, and gets you into flow. Shadow patterns are defined as what will stop you or drain you, mostly by creating inertia.

Using an old movie metaphor, it is like recognizing your Luke Skywalker tendencies and your Darth Vader tendencies (the light and dark side characters from Star Wars).

Lack of self-knowledge of your shadow pattern (dark side) is a major factor in stopping you from realizing your full potential. The more clarity you have about your light and shadow patterns, the easier it will be to recognize your shadow patterns.

Light patterns are those that energize you and get you into flow. ***Examples are:***

trust	enthusiasm
self-esteem	cooperation
generosity	innovation
innocence	perfection
curiosity	manifestation
faith	playfulness
vision	service

Shadow patterns are energy patterns that stop you. **Examples are:**

fear	envy
doubt	competition
obligation	compromise
self-pity	attachment
anxiety	martyrdom
guilt	imitation

All people who successfully manifest their visions recognize—*rapid discovery*—and move past their shadow behavior by having a willingness to switch focus back to lights-on energy—*rapid recovery*. They then go into action by doing any action lighting them up.

> ⊚ **This is a simple truth—if you follow your light, you will get more light, more energy. When you do something that is energizing, you will get more energy. It's that basic.**

Remember the shadow is always there—and it never goes away. The empowerment strategy is to be truthful when you are in your shadow, and quickly shift your attention to your journey. True masters of these principles have learned to embrace both sides, the light and the dark, and move back to the light side as quickly.

Clarity in Action: Terry's Story

Terry, a certified event planner, has a big vision to create an educational and networking venue for women to connect and support their personal and professional growth. Her business includes an annual retreat as well as several other meeting opportunities throughout the year. It is a very complex business that includes arranging the events, contracting with educational speakers and meeting venues, and enrolling sponsors as well as selling memberships. For the first few years, Terry did it all herself with the help of a small group of dedicated volunteers. As the organization grew, Terry became more and more overwhelmed with all that had to be done.

As she began to apply *Get Clarity* concepts to her leadership style and her organization, she became aware of the impact her unconscious shadow behavior was having on her health and effectiveness. She realized her particular shadow behavior was *overdoing*. She had too much on her plate and for years had been doing much of the event work herself, plus taking care of the needs of her family. When she was operating from her shadow of overdoing, she couldn't see any other possibilities for getting everything done. From her perspective, she believed she needed to be doing it all herself. Physically, it was taking a toll. As she began to reflect on how she worked, she realized she often had migraine headaches just as the results of her hard work were being realized.

Terry began to shift her focus to more effective thoughts and behaviors. As a result, she was able to see many different possibilities for more work to be done by others while she still provided her unique leadership perspective to what was being created. This new realization allowed her to focus on trusting others while continually reflecting on how everything could be done from a feeling of *effortlessness*. This shift in her focus has opened her mind to seeing unlimited possibilities and creative strategies. Her business continues to grow and her migraines have almost totally disappeared.

Navigational Tools: Shifting Shadow Patterns

Shifting your thoughts and behaviors from shadow patterns begins with simply noticing where your thoughts and behaviors are. Do you behave above-the-line or below it?

- First, be easy with recognizing your shadow behavior; simply notice where you are— rapid discovery. Where are your thoughts? How are you behaving?

Study the *Get Clarity* Attention Guide found on page 123 for clues.

- Then shift your thoughts above-the-line— rapid recovery. If you are anxious, shift your focus to enthusiasm. Put your attention to thinking about what enthusiasm at this moment would feel like?

- Pay attention to the energy change you feel. Commit to and act from that place. What do you have to do to create enthusiasm? Observe the different result you create and experience.

- You can throw a dart above-the-line and pick any word to focus your attention on. It doesn't have to be the exact opposite of your under-the-line thought.

- What's important is you shifting your thoughts, your behavior and your energy to more effective above-the-line patterns as soon as you notice.

Chapter Thirteen
Embracing Eddies

That's the reason they're called lessons,
because they lessen from day to day.
—Lewis Carroll, Author

Doubt, fear, and well-intended but misguided advice are not the only challenges you are likely to face in navigating your *Get Clarity* journey. As you adjust your course, you are bound to encounter eddies—energetic setbacks that are pictured as whirlpools on the *Get Clarity* Journey Map. An eddy prevents you from moving forward toward your vision by spinning you around and around in place, in a familiar pattern.

Patterns are simply manifestations of lessons you need to learn. Think of a pattern as feedback to help you further your mission and move you away from anything not serving you. An eddy contains information and, therefore, provides a tutorial in a lesson you need to learn.

Lessons tend to be repeated again and again, until you change your response. There's no stigma attached to being caught in an eddy. On the contrary, it's a golden opportunity to experience the pattern in a different way and move closer to mastering the underlying lesson.

When you find yourself swirling around in an eddy, the above-the-line question to ask yourself is, *"What is the lesson here?"* or *"What information am I getting that will help me make a different choice?"* An under-the-line question would be something like, *"What's wrong here?"* or *"Why does this keep happening to me?"* If you focus on what's wrong, you invite self-judgment, criticism, and blame—of others as well as yourself.

A negative focus will seldom give you an answer moving you forward toward your vision.

- Instead of searching for reasons, become an observer.

- Stay curious about your experience.

- Assume nothing.

The less certain you are about what's happening, the more open you will be to seeing all the possibilities. Quantum physics tells us the observer affects what is observed; your thoughts about a situation influence the outcome. So, as much as possible, suspend thinking. Over-reliance on your left-brain analytic skills dulls intuition, a right-brain function. Balancing both sides of the brain will give you access to whole-brain intelligence, sharpening your observation skills.

When you're caught in an eddy, attention and energy are what will keep you afloat so you can recognize patterns no longer serving you; then release them and return to your path.

Practicing gratitude for the opportunity to work through a pattern will also help navigate an eddy with greater ease.

When you finally kick out of an eddy, you will be stronger and wiser for the experience. You will have tapped into deep inner reserves and learned to hold your vision no matter what. The process is not unlike what happens on a real river journey, where the reward for kicking out of an eddy may be uncovering the rich mineral deposits that lie just downstream.

We do a communication exercise in our workshops called pilot/co-pilot. Its purpose is to focus on creating effective communication between people and within and among teams. For the players this exercise almost always points out a less effective communication pattern playing out in their work or personal life.

In a recent workshop as we were debriefing what had occurred, Player #1 said, when she asked for clarification, her partner (Player #2) kept repeating the same words only louder.

Player #2 said her business associates have told her she does this frequently at work, especially under stress. It is an unconscious, patterned response to a request for more clarity about what she was saying.

She immediately wondered why she does that and where she learned it. Asking *"why"* may be informative at some level; however, it does not necessarily provide useful strategies for changing the behavior.

And, it invites judgment and criticism providing little guidance. The question to ask is: *"What is the lesson here?"*

In her case, it was to focus on becoming more conscious, more present, and more self-aware when communicating during times of stress. She determined to create a strategy reminding her of this and raise a red flag to remind her to get present whenever she began to repeat herself in a louder voice.

Clarity in Action: George's Story

George is a team leader in a global consulting company. He takes great pride in being very responsive to his client's needs. When a client calls, George's first reaction is to drop everything and handle this new client emergency. Unfortunately, this reactive pattern exhausts him and burns out his team. George said his career success was built on being responsive and doing whatever was needed to serve the client. However, he was also aware of the pressure this manner of working put on him and his team. It had happened with other teams he led in the past.

George was in the eddy of over-reacting. He determined the lesson he needed to learn was being of co-creative with his team, which involved more than quick responsiveness. He also needed to discover a more effective way of responding to client requests; to have an established team strategy of how to handle the emergency client needs; to delegate more effectively; and to create a communication strategy with his team providing him early notice (like a warning sign) when he slipped into his old pattern.

As a result of being more conscious and paying attention to the pattern, George has created a team approach to more efficiently handle the work, and built systems to create more flow when getting things done. He and his team actually work fewer hours and get more done with reduced pressure.

As you know, changing long-held behaviors and patterns isn't always easy. When the behavior you want to change raises its ugly head once again, you may have a tendency to voice self-judgment and be critical of why you did it again. This is never a successful approach to changing that pattern behavior.

Self criticism is seldom an effective agent of behavior change.

It's important you always express gratitude when you are revisiting a pattern. Practicing gratitude enhances ease and grace. If you are in an eddy revisiting a pattern, you will know you haven't yet learned what you need to learn from a situation or person. In this awareness, be grateful because when the lesson is learned, you may not have to repeat the lesson again.

Clarity in Action: Linda's Story

Linda was a partner in a five-person consulting firm in a metropolitan area. The firm was financially successful largely because she personally conducted the initial client interviews. She had a natural style, a love of meeting people and was a magnet for new business. Attraction marketing was her expertise. Her partners depended on her to bring in new business as well as to consult with clients once they were enrolled.

After several years, however, Linda lost interest in her consultant role. During the *Get Clarity* process she was coached to pay attention and note whenever she felt energized in her work. By staying curious and observing her energy, she noticed that she was very lights-on whenever she was speaking in public and promoting entrepreneurs who had powerful visions.

It became clear what she wanted to do was locate individuals with big visions and coach them in launching their own businesses. With her partners' support, she took a sabbatical from her firm to pursue her interest and opened her own coaching practice.

She expected a decline in income once she went out on her own, but the decline was sharper than anticipated. Since she was responsible for bringing in half of her family's income, the decline caused stress at home. After six months, she realized being on her own was not going to work.

Linda returned to her position at the firm and immediately fell into a familiar behavior pattern— just like falling into an eddy on the Get Clarity Journey Map. Stepping back in was an easy transition, but as she was lulled back into the familiar pattern, it became increasingly harder for her to stay sharp and creative. Linda sensed, however, she was back in the old pattern in order to learn a lesson about being true to herself.

After three months of swirling in that eddy, becoming progressively bored and drained, Linda decided to drop any preconceived ideas about the job and just observe her energy. She shifted her attention to what lit her up, telling herself, *"I'm okay, there's nothing seriously knocking me out here, but I'm falling asleep and that's not okay. What I really want to do aside from public speaking is write a book about brilliant enterprises. I want to honor this calling and be true to myself."*

Linda again resigned from the partnership and started writing. She kicked out of the eddy—and felt stronger and wiser for the experience. Soon thereafter, she found a business partner who wanted to invest in publishing. In addition to publishing books about entrepreneurship, they promote exciting entrepreneurial projects, or as Linda envisioned, *"brilliant enterprises."*

Presently, Linda is doing the public speaking for the firm, and she has published her book on entrepreneurs. She has financial flow, which has improved her family relations, and she is very lights-on about her work.

Clarity in Action— Marcus and Danielle's story

Marcus's experience here is a clear example of how buying love will derail a dream. Marcus has been a company president for most of his life, and his lifestyle is full of luxuries. He is quick and smart, a great problem solver, and a marketing genius for the expansion his company.

However, he seemingly left all of that talent behind at the office when he went home. There confusion reigned with his second wife and their

blended family. Their main problems were a per-
ceived pattern of unequal treatment of their children,
his only daughter and her 2 boys.

Danielle was very jealous of Marcus's daughter
and how Marcus gave preferential treatment to her,
seemingly more than he did to Danielle's children.
He paid for his daughter to attend a posh private
school while refusing to do the same for her children.

He bragged about his daughter's achievements
while minimizing those of her children, as well as
going to his daughter's sports events and missing
the other kids events.

Rather than solving their problems by communicating, Marcus isolated himself by going silent and
withdrawing. Danielle had a confrontive communication style using blame, which often escalated
into yelling. These responses were driving a wedge
between them. They had forgotten the faith that had
brought them together; the faith they could build a
healthier happier family together than they could
have separately as divorced parents.

In the coaching environment, Marcus had to stay
still and listen, and Danielle had to talk clearly and
in a normal tone of voice. Their contentious problems
were scribed onto a large white board (what didn't
work) and their compatible solutions (what did
work) as well.

Over a 2-day period as they talked and listened,
and then looked at the white board as observers, it

was clear that they had a lot of positive shared desires. They embraced the lessons and have continued to show gratitude to each other.

Navigational Tools: Embracing an Eddy

One popular definition of insanity is repeating the same behavior over and over and expecting different results. A classic example is repeatedly getting involved in relationships with the same type of person who always breaks your heart. Another is continually trying to "rescue" people either in relationships or in business, only to be disappointed when things don't go your way. An eddy provides an opportunity to kick an old pattern once and for all.

- Make a list of the patterns you recognize are operating in your life and the lesson or lessons that each represents. Include a list of the patterns you and your partner can experience as well.

- Pick the pattern you feel is most detrimental to your energy and to achieving your vision.

- Create an action step or strategy to break the pattern. Write it down in the form of an intention and make a commitment to taking action to change your approach as an observer. Stay curious, and adopt the beginner's mind: look at all people and situations as if they are brand new to you.

- Practice gratitude. It will help you navigate eddies with ease and grace. Reflect on the lessons you have learned so far on the *Get Clarity* journey. Express gratitude for what you have learned. Be grateful for what you have learned and for the fact that you may not have to repeat the pattern. Write a gratitude statement about each person who has helped you learn those lessons.

PART V

Sail Home

Chapter Fourteen
Staying in the Present

You must live in the present, launch yourself on every wave, find your eternity in each moment. Fools stand on their island opportunities and look toward another land. There is no other land; there is no other life but this.
—Henry David Thoreau, Author and Naturalist

Too often we base our decisions on long-gone events from the past or stories we make up about the future. Staying in present time may seem like a cliché, but realistically, present time is all any of us have—yesterday is gone, and tomorrow isn't here yet. Therefore, it is important to use information from "right now" as your reference point. And if you're truly living in the moment—and reading the energy of your personal and near fields—you'll have all the information needed to make lights-on decisions moving you toward your vision, and ultimately toward living your life purpose, your destiny.

The question is, *how can you stay in present time when your mind is drawn to the past and the future?* Since you've been in flow for a while, one effective way is to continually ask yourself the question, *"What will it take right now to advance our vision?"* Your answer can help you form a revised bridge plan.

Remember: **a bridge plan** is a strategy allowing you and your partner to move from where you are now to where you want to be, while remaining energized, intentional, and clear. ***Bridge-planning*** is a dynamic, on-going process recognizing when your original vision has morphed and you have moved on to Plan B, or C, or D. Actually, you could view a vision-led life as a series of bridge plans, as the river moves you from one spot to the next on your journey.

Only by being awake and aware in present time will you both be able to spot important clues and life lessons as they appear, and see how to connect them. Awareness of what's happening in the moment allows you to experience synchronicity—the concurrence of events meaningfully related—and use that concurrence to your advantage. This is done by seeing how the clues and lessons appearing in your journey fit together to form a picture of your own unique expression, your partnership, and your contribution to the world.

Clarity In Action—Mac and Scott's Story

Mac is a graphic artist who loves symbols and meditates to be able to translate client's words into pictures. Scott is a university professor who has innovated a system to insure words convey the meaning of the pictures Mac designs, a visual vernacular.

Mac and Scott are examples of the perfect template for partnering entrepreneurs—one is highly visionary (right brained and seeing in chaos) and the other is highly strategic (left brained and seeing in order) so together they implement their projects by expanding upon each other's input and taking balanced action from a global perspective.

Both being very admired in their respective disciplines, they let their individual self-importance get the upper hand. They lost sight of the brilliance of their co-created designs. Their business and reputation began to suffer as they veered away from working together to produce unique products to working separately. The divisive energy started to create distance and they noticed that they were repelling each other as well as clients.

In order to regain the successful working style and resultant unique designs, they both had to set aside their egos and focus on authentically working from their strengths. Both realized that they had lost the power of attraction, and they asked for coaching to get them and their design firm back on track.

They began to use the *Get Clarity* check-in as coaching tool to stay awake and in present time, daily both at home and at work. That put positivity before productivity, and as judgment and criticism were dissolved and replaced by respect and gratitude, the flow of attraction began to work, and their problems were resolved.

It is fun to think of your life as a destiny jigsaw puzzle, with the clues as the puzzle pieces. So far on the journey you have sorted through all of the clues, and discarded such lights-off pieces as other people's advice and opinions and your own self-criticism, doubt, fear, and self-defeating patterns. The remaining pieces are your lights-on clues. Linked together, they form a clear picture of the destiny calling you forward. The closer you get to sailing home, you will remember *"home"* means living your life on purpose. The clarity amnesia you started with on this journey has vanished.

Doors open, people appear and opportunities happen when you stay awake and watch for what shows up. Things related to your vision begin to happen very quickly. We call it the *whoosh effect.*

Clarity in Action: John's Story

John is a very successful commercial real estate broker. For many years his biggest vision was to become a developer, building his own office buildings.

With coaching he began to build his bridge plan toward that vision. John had always had a special interest in environmental issues and one of his bridge steps was to learn more about green buildings.

During the following year as he pursued knowledge about green buildings, he began to notice that a few potential commercial tenants were expressing a desire for finding space in green buildings; this was a few years before it became part of the national conversation. After the third person asked the question, John took it as a big clue. He began to quicken and deepen his study. Ultimately, he became LEED certified (Leadership in Energy and Environmental Design).

Continuing on his bridge plan, John purchased his first small office building and did a complete green remodel, becoming the first green real estate developer in his state. He has since added more buildings to his inventory. His lights-on bridge strategy led him to his vision of being a commercial real estate developer even though his original vision did not include doing it green. He followed the clues, stayed present and continued to ask what he could do to serve his vision.

Navigational Tools: Staying Present

Using all of the *Get Clarity* tools—vision mapping, check-in, ritual, holding your energy, Clarity Attention Guides and others—everyday will help you both stay present and allow you each to make effective daily decisions; form clarity for the next steps; and create the appropriate long term strategies.

- At a minimum, ask yourself often *"What worked?"* and *"What didn't work?"* in your performance. **Remember:** *remove judgment and criticism.*

- Make a list of patterns you need to be aware of and be especially watchful for.

- Watch for clues and synchronous events. *Stay curious.* Review the past three months; make note of any clues appearing because they will provide you with something you need.

- Stay objective; don't take any information personally.

- Create a new bridge plan and add more lights-on action steps. Bridge plans are dynamic. They need to be modified frequently, as flow moves you to a new spot on the journey. Place some action steps on the bridge energizing you and will move you closer to your goal with a sense of ease.

Chapter Fifteen
Refreshing Your Vision

Revealing and realizing Noble Purpose is about returning to that which is most essential within you, discovering your perfect wisdom, fulfilling that which seeks expression within you. The journey to Noble Purpose is essentially awakening from your deep sleep to this inner call.
—Dr. Barry Heermann, Author and Educator

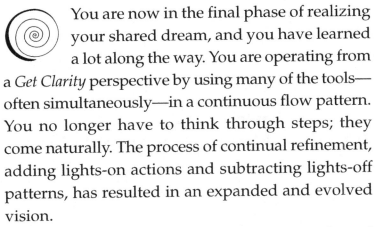 You are now in the final phase of realizing your shared dream, and you have learned a lot along the way. You are operating from a *Get Clarity* perspective by using many of the tools—often simultaneously—in a continuous flow pattern. You no longer have to think through steps; they come naturally. The process of continual refinement, adding lights-on actions and subtracting lights-off patterns, has resulted in an expanded and evolved vision.

When you find yourself stuck momentarily and unable to move forward, you have learned to switch your strategy, adjusting timing or financing or anything else involved in making your dream a reality.

At this point in your journey, you can truly appreciate the wisdom of the saying, *"Life is what happens when you're making other plans"*—and as often as not, it's Plan B. Dreams that are passionate and connected to your hearts take on a life of their own as you continually refine them to keep them viable.

It is obvious by now that some self-reflection is necessary to create a life full of peak experiences; and self-reflection does require taking the time from your daily activities. It can merely be a time out for a few minutes during your daily routine, an hour away from the office or an actual retreat for a few days.

Doing any of these will allow you to reevaluate and refresh your vision and help you discover the strategies needed to align your actions. Taking the time to retreat and refresh is actually being action oriented—it helps you take vision-aligned action.

Navigational Tools: Refresh and Refine Your Shared Vision

Whether you take a week, a day or even a few hours every year, it is important to use the time to reflect on what you have achieved toward your shared vision and set an intention for the coming year, one with both of your lights-on actions in mind. One approach is a reflective retreat—which we find to be very effective—it's an annual version of the *Get Clarity* daily check-in. If you do this every year, you will be energized by how much has been accomplished when you review your old notes together.

Upon review, ask each of these questions for each of the fields, yours, mine, and ours.

- What's different in the past year? What did you achieve towards your vision? What aligned actions have you taken? Acknowledge all that you have accomplished on your leadership journey.

- What worked in the past year in your performance? Be sure to fully acknowledge and appreciate all that you did to improve your performance. Look back at all of the principles you incorporated into your way of being every day. Make a list of all of your actions, thoughts and behaviors that worked. This is a time to acknowledge your performance and celebrate your accomplishments.

- What could you have done differently to be more effective? As you know, this is not a place for self-judgment or criticism. Merely list the facts of your year 's performance and what could have been done more effectively.

What are some strategies you can incorporate into your daily life to address these less effective behaviors in the coming year?

- What is the state of your mind? At this time of annual reflection, what is the state of your mind? Is your mind clear, open, and anticipating the wonder and possibilities of the year to come?

- What is the state of your body? Are you physically comfortable? Are you healthy and fit? Are there areas of stress or discomfort that you need to create strategies to address in the coming year?

- What is the state of your spirit as you approach the next year? Is it light, grateful, expansive, or creative? Let your intuition and your intention access the state of your spirit as you envision what you want for the coming year.

- What are you grateful for? What has happened in the past year that fills you with gratitude at this reflective moment in time? Who are the people who have enriched your experiences this year? Do you have gratitude

for all the lessons you have learned this
year? Do you feel gratitude for the
abundance and flow you have experienced?
Is there gratitude for the opportunities you
have as this new year begins?

- What is your intention? What are your most
  expansive intentions for the coming year?
  Where do you want to put your focus and
  your aligned actions? Where can you be the
  most effective to achieving your vision?

- Create a new vision map. This annual check-
  in will help you refine and refresh your
  vision. Look at all that you have noted and
  make a list of anything that can be added to
  your expanding vision. What do you want to
  add to your most expansive desires for your
  work and your life? Add these to your new
  vision map.

Chapter Sixteen

Plunging into Your Destiny

*You must give birth to your images. They are the future
waiting to be born. Fear not the strangeness that you feel.
The future must enter you long before it happens.
Just wait for the hour, the birth of new clarity.*
—Rainer Maria Rilke, German Poet

Everything is perfect, and as it should be—that is our belief. But sometimes what shows up initially may not look perfect to you at the time. However, by releasing the outcome—your willful picture of how you think it should look—you allow for serendipity to provide your perfect solution. Once you have successfully let go of your attachment to a certain outcome you will be able to say, *"I was clear about my intention, and what showed up is perfect."*

There is a formula to follow for getting what you want and manifesting your dream. It involves using all the tools you have learned on your *Get Clarity journey.*

The Formula:
Intention + Attention + Action + Release the Outcome = Manifestation of Your Vision.

Intention: You set your intention having a clear, lights-on vision for what you want, individually and together as a partnership. You write down your visions, stating fully what you want—*not what you don't want*. It is also important to have a visual representation of your shared vision to remind both of you of what you want: vision maps, lists of lights-on clues, and bridge plans are all part of setting your intention—and keeping them in present time by using the visual.

Attention: You focus your attention on creating your shared vision. What you focus on expands, gaining more and more of your attention, so you need to focus only on what you want. Allow yourself time to visualize often what you want to create. Using rapid discovery and rapid recovery will help you keep your attention on what you are creating.

Action: You step directly into action aligned with your vision, following the lights-on action steps on your bridge plan. The action steps must energize you, so your experience as an energy detective will help you discern which action steps to take yourself and which ones to delegate to others. Watch for clues: Is there effort involved in what you're doing, or does it flow easily? High noticing and observing resistance will serve you well here.

Release the outcome: Putting all your energy into forcing the results you want will keep you from seeing a better version of your dream if that's what appears. Practice the mantra: *"I was clear about my intention, and what showed up is perfect"*— whatever it is.

Manifestation of your vision: When you hold your personal energy field and don't revert to old patterns, vision-to-outcome happens rapidly. In *Get Clarity* terms, the very short time gap between envisioning an outcome and its actual occurrence is known as the *"whoosh effect."* In some cases, the result is instantaneous. So fasten your seat belt and be very clear about what you ask for!

Clarity in Action— Matt and Lilly's story

This is the perfect last client story on the river. It's an example of moving from very good to great by enhancing an already lights-on partnership.

Matt and Lilly realized their pattern of overdoing was draining their co-creative energy. As a married couple working together in their professional practice, leading a staff of eight, parenting two young children, being active in the community, their life was very full. On a scale of 1–10, they ranked their life as very good (7). They chose *Clarity* coaching to get a refreshed vision for how to stay energized and move their life to great (10).

An important part of moving to great involved a decision to expand their professional practice to include new therapies that excited both of them. At this choice point, it was clear they needed to take a retreat, away from the fast pace of their life, and co-create a vision for their future. Knowing that adding without subtracting was a formula for exhaustion, their first step was for each of them to separately choose what actions they were willing to release. They looked at the issues of more delegation to office staff as well as hiring help for household duties. The process was so useful, Lilly felt lighter for eliminating the duties that were lights-off. As they moved things off his list, Matt just felt a huge relief of the pressure that had been bothering his stomach.

Their next step was focusing on what was lights-on for them individually, and then combine their common lights-on visions as partners—creating their shared expansive vision. Following the *Clarity* process, they focused on three energy fields—a Lilly field, a Matt field and the shared field. From this exercise, focused and clear lights-on actions steps were created. One year later, being disciplined about daily check-ins with each other, and implementing the action steps, they broke ground on their new office. They are energized, co-creative and report that they are living life at a magnificent 10.

Navigational Tools: Be Clear

Matt and Lilly's story perfectly illustrates the benefits of being very clear about your intentions in all aspects of your vision.

- Keep your focus fully engaged on what you want and stay conscious of where your thoughts are.

- Step into aligned action immediately and be observant of the energy flow.

- Release the outcome and joyfully watch what shows up in response to your intention.

- Notice how quickly your vision manifests. Often, it happens as soon as you think it. If you are still unclear what role synchronicity can play in manifesting your vision, keep track of "coincidences" as they occur in your life. Keep a synchronicity journal. Note how the concurrence of a dream or thought or feeling with an external event moves you in the direction of your vision.

- Hold on to your hat and relish the rapid acceleration of the whoosh effect!

Chapter Seventeen
Living Lights-On

*You are what your deep driving desire is. As your desire is,
so is your will. As your will is, so is your deed. As your
deed is, so is your destiny.*
—Upanishads, ancient Indian text

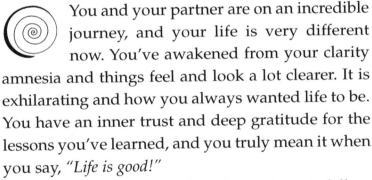 You and your partner are on an incredible
journey, and your life is very different
now. You've awakened from your clarity
amnesia and things feel and look a lot clearer. It is
exhilarating and how you always wanted life to be.
You have an inner trust and deep gratitude for the
lessons you've learned, and you truly mean it when
you say, *"Life is good!"*

You and your partner both know how to follow
clues and live a *"loving what you do"* and *"doing what
you love"* lifestyle. You are able to value both the
peaks and the valleys of your relationships.

Challenging events earlier in the *Get Clarity*
journey which might have seemed catastrophic—
divorce, death of a loved one, illness or injury, job

loss—now appear as opportunities for revisioning, learning, and growth instead of dramatics. Regardless of what happens, you and your partner are now able to continue along your lights-on path. From this point forward, there is no going back and living your life the old way. Going forward, your journey and relationships are illuminated and purposeful.

Knowing *"your lights are an inside job"*, you now realize it's not your job or your mission to hold your partner's energy for them, but to support and assist them in living lights-on.

On the *Get Clarity* Journey map, you have parked your boat, symbolizing the end of this phase of your journey. You no longer need the boat to carry you along in the flow. This ending marks a new beginning. Your feet are on the ground, and your backpacks are filled with heart-connected wisdom and energy tools to guide and keep you on the path. You have *"cracked the Get Clarity code"* by learning you must always use your heart energy, not just the power of your intellect, to guide you.

Old thinking patterns have dissolved. Over-analyzing, without also observing your energy, no longer serves you, and you've become intrinsically aware of it. Your individual and shared visions are linked to your passions, which produces a powerful chain reaction of energy—an acceleration effect. And you can feel when heart connection occurs.

As you come to this phase of the *Get Clarity* journey, manifestation is rapid. You envision something and it shows up. Being able to both notice and celebrate this for yourself and your partner is a vital step in keeping up your "whoosh" effect. In honoring your own distinct and unique energy patterns, you know you're following guidance instead of your will.

Your energy remains constant, and you'll stay lights-on more and more. It's important to be able to recognize the energy signals in yourself and in your partner; reflecting back to them when they're living lights-on will help you both stay there more often. There is a noticeable increase in your vitality and, simultaneously, a feeling of ease and peace. People who meditate call it *"restful awareness,"* and you live your life in that state every day.

You've personally left behind your old, indecisive ways as well as the ineffective ways not working in your relationships.

At choice points you choose intentionally and create clear outcomes. No more accidental bumping around in your life. Your journey forward is transformed with passion and purpose.

There are so many more stories of transformation we can tell you, and we wish we had room to tell them all. They are stories of everyday heroes and heroines who have courageously faced coming undone and then reforming in a new and more passionate way, to live their dreams: an architect who became a country music composer; a real estate developer who became an expert in overseas relocations; a PhD scientist who became a blues singer; a concierge who became a seminar leader; a financial advisor who became an internet marketing advisor; a nutritionist who became an equine-assisted therapist; a bookseller who became a retreat-center owner.

And there are just as many stories of partners who used the *Get Clarity* journey to refresh their visions and revitalize their energy and partnerships: a business owner who found a new love for her company rather than sell it; a couple on the verge of divorce who found loving power in holding their own energy; a therapist who gained a new connection with her patients; business partners who were in conflict and found a new way to work together seamlessly; a divorcing couple who gained new guidelines to stay positive for their teenaged daughter. Like the people whose stories we've included in the book, they've made the changes you dream of.

They are couples, partners and individuals now living each day, happily free of judgment or criticism. They continue to create their reality by making daily lights-on choices and choose energizing actions moving them forward toward their bigger vision. They're attracting what they want into their life energetically and focusing their attention on manifesting magnificent lives.

They look younger and brighter, feel healthier, and love what they're doing. In short, this is the definition of lights-on living.

When you started this journey, the river seemed long, and the prospect might have been overwhelming. Now you've arrived at the end, scaled the mountain, and are looking down, the river seems less formidable, and you are grateful it has carried you along to safety. From this vantage point, it's easy to see the rewards of making this heroic journey: remembrance of your destiny and calling; understanding of the shared vision; an embodied process in which you've learned to create new inspired visions and effective strategies; and the knowledge to sustain the journey through the peaks and valleys as your life continues to unfold.

As the poet T.S. Eliot wrote, *"To make an end is to make a beginning. The end is where we start from."*

Appendix
Post Partnership

There will be times you have to leave what you don't want behind in order to be in the right place to find what you do want.
—Theresa Byrne

Breaking up is hard to do, no doubt about it. No one signs up to start a partnership dreaming of the ending. There will be times, no matter how much you want it to work, when a relationship or partnership isn't meant to last. Sometimes there are too many under-the-line things not working for partners to remain together. Or the negative aspects of a business outweigh the positive and it's time to dissolve it. In this book, we've discussed the *third energy field (ours)*, and if this energy between two people becomes negative and it's not shifting, it may mean it's time to consider an ending.

No one starts a relationship or partnership with an end in mind; we're too excited about the possibilities of what we can create together. But the reality is this: over 50% of marriages end in divorce (over 67% of 2nd marriages, 73% of 3rd marriages) and 90% of businesses fail in the first five years. We don't want to think about the end when we start, but what if we learned the skills necessary to make any ending a positive experience? What if we weren't afraid of breakups or dissolutions and it created an opening instead?

We hear about it all the time, couples having a nasty breakup or divorcing and trying to *"take each other to the cleaners"*. Business partners going to battle against one another for the domain of a company. Even friends once seeming inseparable who now can't stand to be in the same room, and make sure to undermine their former friend to anyone who'll listen.

All that battling, fighting, attacking, or conniving energy doesn't have a place in lights-on living; it's draining, exhausting, and wrecks havoc on the body and immune systems.

There is another way.

There's a way to dissolve any type of partnership, whether it's a friendship, romantic relationship, or business partnership and stay committed to a greater vision serving both parties.

The goal of this Appendix is to offer you some ideas on how to *"come undone"*.

Should I Stay or Should I Go?

Too often people stay together out of need, obligation, fear, or doubt about what a future without the other person might look like. Based on this kind of *"under-the-line"* thinking, our shadow behaviors and actions would naturally start to show up. Things like insecurity, jealousy, playing small, getting stuck in drama, and negativity.

It would be nice if there were a T Chart of pros and cons to let us know if it was time for a partnership to end, but that would only keep us stuck in our heads.

Cleaning Up Your Relationship Karma

You've probably heard of the concept of past lives, and that each person is completing lessons and growth from a prior life in this one.

In the same vein, what if we carry energy and unfinished business from each of our past partnerships forward into the next one? What if we don't learn what we need to learn so we can move on and forward? What if we just continually drag our baggage with us as if it was some kind of designer luggage?

In many second and third marriages one of the catalysts for divorce is a partner who may not have recovered from the last breakup, and moved into the new relationship without taking enough time to recover and get their own vision and priorities straight— and learn the valuable lessons necessary for them to grow.

By cleaning up your relationship karma, you are no longer held hostage by the old patterning and can freely move forward into the vision you've created for yourself using the navigational tools learned in this book.

So how do you clear up your relationship karma?

- Take time between relationships to move back from yours, mine, and ours.

- Learn what is yours. Learn what is your partner's.

- Heal. Most endings come with a feeling of grief. Allowing the grief to process through your system will help you in moving forward.

- Look at what you've learned in the relationship. Even negative-appearing lessons can have great value.

- Re-evaluate what matters to you; what lights you up, what brings you joy, and what you love to do.

- Begin to create a new vision. (Use the *Get Clarity* visioning exercise in this book as a place to start creating).

- Create inspired action steps toward making the new vision a reality.

Gratitude For the Lessons

In each relationship you are there to learn something; or be shown something—it might be about yourself, your partner, the world, or any number of potential categories. The best way to figure out what the lessons are is to ask a few powerful questions.

The questions to ask yourself:

"What did I learn from this relationship?"
"What didn't I know but now I do?"
"What have I learned which will help me going forward?"
"What did this person/partnership teach me or show me?"

Even if a lesson appears negative on the outset, you still learned something. Maybe you learned to be more discerning; maybe you learned to check in on the finances more often; maybe you learned to trust your gut instinct. All of these are valuable lessons.

Courageous Conversations

"Courage" means acting in the face of fear, even when fear is present. Having tough conversations takes courage because at the most basic level it gets you out of homeostasis, internal stability, and the ease of status quo.

This is one reason so many people avoid having these hard conversations; it's incredibly emotionally difficult. At its core, the most basic human-to-human need is to seek connection and avoid rejection; a drive allowing for the survival of our species for many years when we lived in tribal communities. A potentially dividing conversation triggers parts of our ancient programming, but stuffing down feelings isn't workable either.

Just thinking about having to bring up some-thing not working with someone you care about is enough to strike fear in even the most enlightened of beings. Some of the most terrifying moments for any of us are typically when we have to address something conflicting or talk about problems.

Being able to have these conversations outside of all the fears, negative thoughts, and emotions, which may show up, is a practice. It's a boundary in being able to talk about what you want and what you need, as well as what's *not working*. The flip side of having respectful boundaries is learning how to have positive connecting conversation, even when a boundary has been crossed.

One of the most challenging courageous conversations is the break up talk. Whether you're the "breaker", or the "breakee," it's all a challenge. If you're the one who wants to get out of a partnership, it can be difficult because you feel like a bad person, and fear hurting the other. If you're the "breakee" it's natural to have feelings like blame or guilt, but they'll never make you actually feel better.

The best way to have a courageous conversation is to consider what you'd like to bring up, and make sure to keep blame or any other lights-off states out of it. Find a good time to talk, and ask your partner if it is a good time to bring up some things on your mind. Then share how you're feeling, and what you'd like to see be different in the relationship.

Leaving with Grace

The best way to describe this is to tell you another story.

Theresa, after noticing an interesting energy present in a lovely year and a half relationship, asked the man an important question, *"Do you see us moving more into partnership in the future? Is it something you want?"*

It took courage to ask those questions. It's never easy bringing up a difficult conversation; it's the kind no one wants to have. She was really proud of herself for addressing it. There were some things not working for her, and in deciding what and how to discuss these all these things she needed to understand where he was coming from.

His immediate answer was, *"I don't know. Can I think about it? Right now I can't plan anything further than next week, or the next vacation."* Which gave her a good idea where he was. She told him to simmer on it for a week.

The next week they had "The Talk" and broke off the relationship. After they agreed to break apart, he was expecting a certain amount of dramatic reaction. However, Theresa said, *"I want to thank you for everything you brought into my life. You've been such a joy to be with over these past years, and I don't regret a single moment. It's been an honor to share "Big Love" with you. I wouldn't change a thing. You've meant so much to me, I'm glad I fell in love with you and part of me will always love you. I wish you every happiness going forward, and I hope you can look back at this relationship and smile because you've made me smile and laugh really loudly many, many times. Thank you."*

Grace means it's possible to move past the feelings of anger, resentment, hurt, and anxiety and a desire to hurt the person we're ending with.

If you choose to live a lights-on life you know everything happening is for your highest and best, even if you can't make sense of it yet. Yes, Theresa was hurt, and knew she would cry when she was alone, and it would take some time to heal her heart. The difference was in knowing none of it was her ex-partner's fault. It's just what happens when relationships end.

There are ways to share your upsets with grace, and there are ways to end relationships in grace; you just have to be open to trying.

Moving Forward

After applying the tips in this chapter, it will make moving forward after a relationship much cleaner for both of you.

Without taking the relationship karma with you, by treating your partner with respect, by having courageous conversations with them, by being grateful of what you've learned from the relationship, it allows you to leave with grace.

Then you can focus on getting your own energy field back to where you need it to be, filling yourself up with all the things lighting you up. In letting go of the "ours" field, it's natural to experience grief as part of the reorganization process. Allow it to happen, allow yourself time to heal and eventually you will once again be ready for a powerful partnership.

Clarity in Action— Jackson and Diana's story

Jackson and Diana are a successful example of positive divorce, coming undone with intention. Jackson, an architect, was handling the stress of his work by coming home and relaxing with several cocktails.

Diana, a home based entrepreneur, noticed that he was coming home earlier & earlier and drinking more and more. Their daughter noticed this behavior and began to become uncomfortable because her Dad was no longer interested in participating in her after school activities.

After several years, the dysfunction forced Diana to make the heart-wrenching decision to divorce. While Jackson agreed there was a problem, making and breaking multiple promises to quit drinking unsuccessfully, he wouldn't do anything to change it.

During that time, most of their attention was focused on their differences and placing blame on the active drinker. Realizing parenting their daughter was the vision bigger than their individual differences, they decided to divorce by creating a shared vision of how they would do it.

In coaching they created a plan for shared parenting. The co-parenting plan and the action steps on dividing property, communication strategies and parenting were all steps giving them the ability to have the "difficult" conversation with their daughter and have her input into the planning. Now several years later, they are still a family even though both parents have married others. They and their daughter continue to adhere to the shared vision they had for being a loving, lights-on divorced family.

Navigational Tools: Breaking Up with Intention

Jackson and Diana ended their marriage with intention and grace, allowing their relationship as parents to grow into something different and still lights-on.

- Clean up your relationship karma. Take the time to create a shared vision for the future. Then take time to create new individual visions.

- Express gratitude for the lessons learned.

- Leave with grace and gratitude for the experience.

Glossary

Above the Line: A way of being that is energetically more effective, consisting of thoughts and behaviors that help you shift your attention and focus to making choices that are energizing, passionate, and solution-focused.

Biofield, or Energy Field: A matrix of energies that extends outward from the body and interacts with the energy fields of other people and the environment, providing a constant exchange and feedback of information.

Bridge Plan: A strategy with actions designed to move you from where you are now to where you want to go.

Cellular Learning: Learning that takes place internally, at a deep, physiological level.

Choice Point: A key moment on the Clarity journey when two or more divergent channels appear, offering an opportunity to make a decision that is energizing or draining.

Energy: An invisible force or current. In the body, it is the force of vitality, also known as life force, chi, ki, prana, and élan vital.

Energy Language: A metaphorical vernacular used to describe life force as it is seen and sensed. On the Clarity journey, the expressions *"lights-on"* and *"that lights you up"* convey the psycho-physical feeling of being passionate and energized, while "lights-off" refers to a feeling of being drained

Energy Meter: A means of calibrating how lights-on (energizing) or lights-off (draining) a person, place, or situation is.

Energy Pattern: An energy cluster in the personal energy field manifesting as a psychological complex or pattern of behavior.

Energy Scan: A very rapid assessment of approach or avoidance, used when encountering an unfamiliar person or environment.

High Noticing: Tuning in to energetic signals and vitality clues in yourself and your environment.

Law of Attraction: Energetic principle by which thoughts, words, and actions generate a force field of energy that draws an equal force field in return.

Lights-off: A low-energy, drained feeling that often appears as a dull or glazed look in the eyes.

Lights-on: An energized feeling that manifests as a look of radiance and vitality—an overall glow and a twinkle in the eye.

Monkey Mind: An inner voice that provides nonstop, self-critical, judgmental chatter.

Near Field: Your immediate surroundings—including home, family, office, automobile, neighborhood, and community—with which your personal energy field interacts continually.

Personal Field: The energetic space around you, extending an arm's length from your body, that receives information (feedback) from the near field.

Personal GPS: Inner guidance, or an instinctive knowing of what energizes and drains you.

Rapid Discovery: Speedy recognition of draining energy patterns.

Rapid Recovery: Speedy utilization of strategies to regain your energy.

Remote Field: The energy field most distant from you, over which you have little or no control.

Under the Line: A way of being that is energetically less effective, consisting of thoughts and behavior patterns that are energy-draining and problem-focused.

Vision: An image clearly seen in the imagination that creates a possibility for the future.

References and Bibliography

Briggs, John, and Peat, David. *Seven Lessons of Chaos—Spiritual Wisdom From the Science of Change.* New York: Harper Collins, 1999.

Buckingham, Marcus, and Coffman, Curt. *First, Break All The Rules.* New York: Simon & Schuster, 1999.

Campbell, Joseph. *The Power of Myth.* New York: Anchor Books, 1991.

Collinge, William. *Subtle Energy—Awakening to the Unseen Forces in Our Lives.* New York: Warner Books, 1998.

Collins, Jim. *Good to Great.* New York: Harper Collins, 2001.

Csikszentmihalyi, Mihaly. *Flow—The Psychology of Optimal Experience. New* York: Harper & Row, 1990.

Dyer, Dr. Wayne W. *The Power of Intention.* California: Hay House, 2004.

Emerald, David. *The Power of TED, The Empowerment Dynamic.* Washington: Polaris Publishing, 2006.

Hawkins, David. *Power vs. Force—The Hidden Determinates of Human Behavior.* California: Hay House, 1995.

Heerman, Barry. *Noble Purpose*. Virginia: QSU Publishing, 2004.

Heider, John. *The Tao of Leadership*. Georgia: Humanics New Age, 1985.

Hock, Dee. *The Birth of the Chaordic Age*. California: Berrett-Koehler, 1999.

Klein, Eric, and Izzo, John. *Awakening Corporate Soul*. Canada: Fairwinds Press, 1998.

Lapid-Bogda, Ginger. *Bringing Out the Best in Yourself at Work*. New York: McGraw Hill, 2004.

LeVoy, Gregg. *Callings—Finding and Following and Authentic Life*. New York: Harmony Books, 1997.

Lipton, Bruce. *The Biology of Belief*. California: Mountain of Love/Elite Books, 2005.

McTaggart, Lynne. *The Field—The Quest for the Secret Force of the Universe*. New York: Harper Collins, 2002.

Pink, Daniel. *A Whole New Mind; Moving from the Information Age to the Conceptual Age*. New York: Riverhead Books, 2005.

Roam, Dan. *The Back of the Napkin: Solving Problems and Selling Ideas with Pictures*. New York: Penguin Group, 2008.

Schwartz, Jeffrey, M.D., and Begley, Sharon. *The Mind & The Brain: Neuroplasicity and the Power of Mental Force*. New York: Regan Books, 2002.

Seligman, Martin. *Learned Optimism: How to Change Your Mind*. New York: Free Press, 1990.

Toms, Michael, and Justine Willis. *True Work—The Sacred Dimension of Earning a Living*. New York: Bell Tower, 1998.

Whyte, David. *Crossing the Unknown Sea, Work as a Pilgrimage of Identity*. New York: Riverhead Books, 2001.

Jaworski, Joseph. *Synchronicity, The Inner Path of Leadership*. California: Berrett-Koehler, 1996.

The Authors

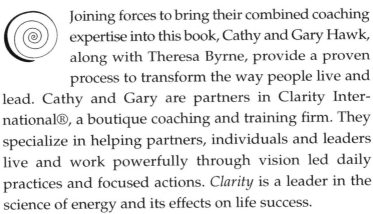Joining forces to bring their combined coaching expertise into this book, Cathy and Gary Hawk, along with Theresa Byrne, provide a proven process to transform the way people live and lead. Cathy and Gary are partners in Clarity International®, a boutique coaching and training firm. They specialize in helping partners, individuals and leaders live and work powerfully through vision led daily practices and focused actions. *Clarity* is a leader in the science of energy and its effects on life success.

Theresa Byrne is an entrepreneur, self defense Master Instructor, and mentor who founded a new way of leading in martial arts. She's also the creator of InPower Living; a biodynamic boundary system, which helps, people fully harness and utilize their inner power. She is a Certified Shift Facilitator in the *Get Clarity* Operating System.

Based on almost 25 years of proven results with individuals, partners and teams, the *Clarity* approach presents a visioning, leadership and communication model that is powerful, repeatable and sustainable. This innovative process heightens and clarifies innate skills of tuning in to energetic signals and vitality clues that are constantly being sent and received in everyone's life and work. *Clarity* clients focus on the energetic actions appropriate to their vision and clearly see what needs to be done to achieve it.

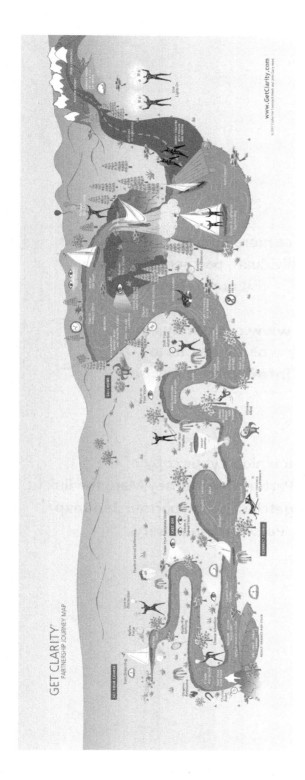

To download your copy of the Get Clarity® Partnership Journey Map, the link is: http:www.getclarity.com/partnership-map/.

Password: getclarity.

To find out more about Clarity programs
for individuals, partners and teams
visit our website:

www.getclarity.com
or contact us at
info@getclarity.com

To download your copy of the
Get Clarity® Partnership Journey Map, the link is:
http:www.getclarity.com/partnership-map/.
Password: getclarity.

Made in the USA
Las Vegas, NV
08 May 2021